HANS MAGNUS ENZENSBERGER

TUMULT

Translated by Mike Mitchell

Seagull
BOOKS

LONDON NEW YORK CALCUTTA

This publication has been supported by a grant
from the Goethe-Institut India

Seagull Books, 2022

First published in German as *Tumult* by Hans Magnus Enzensberger
© Suhrkamp Verlag Berlin, 2014

First published in English by Seagull Books, 2016
English translation © Mike Mitchell, 2016

Published as part of the Seagull Library of German Literature, 2022

ISBN 978 1 8030 9 044 3

British Library Cataloguing-in-Publication Data
A catalogue record for this book is available from the British Library

Typeset by Seagull Books, Calcutta, India
Printed and bound by WordsWorth India, New Delhi, India

CONTENTS

NOTES ON A FIRST ENCOUNTER WITH RUSSIA

(1963)

The address wasn't quite correct but the letter still made it to my letter box: Budal Gar, Tome, Norway. The Italians always have a problem with letters that don't exist in their alphabet. I couldn't immediately decipher the sender's name on the back of the envelope. It consisted of an abbreviation: *Comes*. 'Caro amico,' I read; the man who addressed me in such a friendly manner was called Giancarlo Vigorelli and signed as general secretary and editor of the Roman periodical, *L'Europa Letteraria*. Only then did I remember that I had met him years ago. A talent such as his is not that rare in Italy. Ambition, skill and good connections across the whole range of political parties allowed him access to funds—the origins of which remained unclear. He used them to establish an organization that called itself the Comunitá Europea degli Scrittori. Malicious tongues compared him to an impresario or a circus ringmaster, but that was unfair, his enterprises were commendable. In the middle of the Cold War, there was no one else who put so much energy and geniality into trying to bridge the gulf between the hostile blocks, at least in the cultural field. In this way, he had already brought about the occasional get-together between 'Western' and 'Eastern' writers.

Now I had an invitation from him to a meeting that was to be held in Leningrad. It wasn't clear to me how I'd come to be on Vigorelli's list. For, as he intimated, it contained authors from many countries, including some high-profile names. It was certainly not a matter of course that Vigorelli should take West Germans into consideration. For us Leningrad was mythical, not to say forbidden territory that was not in the Near, but the Far East. On the one hand, this was because only 20 years ago a German army had encircled the city, besieged and starved it out, and on the other, because Yalta had made the city disappear behind a curtain that was difficult to open. The mood on either side of the Wall was militant, made toxic by the fear of escalation on the join between the two empires.

Germany was two protectorates: on the one side, the lukewarm Federal Republic and on the other, the 'Zone', about which I had few illusions, having been inoculated against it by the evidence of what I had seen and by my early reading of Hannah Arendt's *The Origins of Totalitarianism*, George Orwell's *Homage to Catalonia* and Czeslaw Milosz's *The Captive Mind*. I had also acquired a modicum of basic knowledge of

Marxism with the help of a Jesuit from Freiburg. That was Gustav Wetter who, in two volumes, dissected Dialectical Materialism as carefully as a cannibal would an infant he wanted to consume. He was allowed to do that in the middle of the Cold War, and much of what the vivisection brought to light made sense to me. But what I still needed and books could not provide, was the autopsy. I wanted to see with my own eyes how things were on the other side, not only in the satellite provinces but in Russia, that for a long time had just been called *CCCP*, the Union of Soviet Socialist Republics.

Thus it came about on an August afternoon—I can still remember that it was a Saturday—I landed in Leningrad on a Russian plane. Jean-Paul Sartre and Simone de Beauvoir, Nathalie Sarraute, Angus Wilson, William Golding, Giuseppe Ungaretti and Hans Werner Richter had made the trip while on the Eastern side Mikhail Sholokhov, Ilya Ehrenburg, Konstantin Fedin, Aleksandr Tvardovsky, Yevgeny Yevtushenko, Jerzy Putrament from Poland and Tibor Déry from Hungary were there. Someone from the GDR had turned up as well, a certain Hans Koch, of whom all that was known was that he was secretary of the East German Writers' Association. Ingeborg Bachmann had been invited but had called off at the last minute and on no account did East German and Russian officialdom want to have Uwe Johnson there.

Nevertheless, they presumably still needed the odd German from the Federal Republic, for the outside world had gradually lifted the political quarantine that we were under. But whom? Max Frisch would have been better, however, he was Swiss. But wasn't there that well-known figure, Hans Werner Richter? Word of the saga of Gruppe 47 had even got as far as Moscow. The official topic for debate was anodyne: 'Problems of the contemporary novel'. But then why me, who had never written a novel? I think that it was, above all, my date of birth that had swung the decision. They could rest assured that there would not be any awkward revelations from the Nazi period; moreover, I was considered to be vaguely 'left-wing'—whatever that means.

I'd never been to Russia before. I wasn't familiar with the habits and customs there. Since the Soviet Writers' Association had taken over the organization, we were considered a delegation, not to say, guests of the state. We were put up in the best hotel in the city, right on Nevsky Prospect. In the foyer were handwoven carpets from the Caucasus, from Bokhara and Persia, and in the overheated bathrooms huge tubs with cast-iron lion's feet. There was also a winter garden with palm trees. With its somewhat shabby splendour, its chandeliers and massive desks, the great hotel was no longer frequented by gentlemen such as

Turgenev and Tchaikovsky or, later on, a Gorky or a Mayakovsky but was catering for a new class of guests.

A small kiosk was selling newspapers in many languages, but I had to make do with Communist Party papers such as *Neues Deutschland*, *L'Unità* and *L'Humanité*—I couldn't even decipher the titles of the others. Was that Mongolian, Armenian or Tajik? In that situation I preferred to stick to *Pravda*, for even my paltry Russian was enough to understand the headlines, because it was easy to guess what they were proclaiming: successes in agricultural and industrial production, bad news from the capitalist world. My request for a street map was met with incomprehension. In fact, no one seemed interested in maps at all, and simply to ask for one aroused astonishment—only spies sought to obtain such state secrets.

To make up for that, our 'delegation' (consisting solely of its leader, Hans Werner Richter, and myself) had two escorts at our disposal and they quickly turned out to be a piece of undeserved good fortune. The function of these guides is, of course, mainly to act as interpreters, to help stuttering foreigners get by, but they do have other duties as well—they had to protect not only the guest but also the state from embarrassment. Their superiors expect them to report on how the visitors behave and what they think. One of them was Lev Ginzburg, an easy-going man, a highly qualified Germanist and translator who had presumably been allotted this task only on a temporary basis. The other one, Konstantin Bogatyrev, didn't seem too bothered about his official duties either, waving away ideological claptrap like annoying flies. Indeed, he was soon saying such derogatory things about the ruling party and its leaders that I wondered whether we had been lumbered with an agent provocateur. Given the omnipresent surveillance, the idea did not seem unreasonable but I soon came to realize that my suspicion was unfounded.

Kostya—as he called himself—was a slightly built, almost undernourished man of 30 or 35, you could tell just by looking at him that he had been through some hard times. He knew the system inside out, knew what punishments and privileges you had to be on the look-out for, which shops were there for the favoured few and what different levels of privilege there were. When I asked him how his teeth came to be damaged, he replied, casually, that they were a souvenir from his time in the prison camp. Bit by bit, he told me, as if it was nothing out of the ordinary, about the convicts among whom he had spent a few years there, far beyond the Urals. Since then he had got to know all about dentists. That turned out to be helpful because overnight Hans Werner developed toothache that put him out of action for two days.

Kostya's true passion wasn't for politics, but for poetry. Perhaps that was what had got him into trouble, perhaps, he'd copied out forbidden poems and passed them on. That was suggested by the fact that he could recite Osip Mandelstam's poems by heart as well as Rilke's *Duino Elegies*—and those even in German.

That kind of thing had always been typical of the Russian intelligentsia. Kostya was the embodiment of the ethos of people for whom literature means more than anything else, a cult that has long since vanished from our part of the world.

What even I knew was that that neglected beauty, Saint Petersburg—Petro- or Leningrad—was a place where every street corner was haunted by literary ghosts. But Pushkin, Tolstoy, Gogol, Dostoyevsky, the Serapion Brothers and writers such as Velimir Khlebnikov and Daniil Kharms did not feature in the debates on the agenda the Congress had arranged.

Konstantin Fedin, an influential man, chairman of the virtually all-powerful Writers' Association, had a go at Joyce, Proust and Kafka; the French defended the *nouveau roman*, and the functionaries praised Socialist Realism. All of which was very tedious. Only Ilya Ehrenburg, who, in spirit if not in name, led the Soviet delegation, brought some life into the proceedings. There was no surprise in that, for back in 1954 with his short novel *The Thaw* he'd initiated the first tentative period of criticism of Stalinism. He got on the nerves of the old guard of the association with that. 'Our writers,' he said, 'don't write bad novels because they speak up for socialism but because the good Lord has not blessed them with talent. There's no Tolstoy, no Dostoyevsky, no Chekhov in sight anywhere in the Soviet Union. But we do have a sufficiency of untalented authors.' It was true, he went on, there had to be writers who appealed to the millions, but Russian literature also needed others who only wrote for 5,000 readers. He had to say that he could make nothing of the *nouveau roman* which had been highly praised, but we all ought to respect the right to experiment. That was the high point of the discussion.

No one went back to his argument, not even Ehrenburg himself. Man of the world that he was, he preferred to chat about Germany with Hans Werner. He even made time for me, despite the fact that I was completely unknown in Russia.

But, after all, a congress is just a congress, so whenever possible Kostya and I went AWOL. Our time for this was very limited. We had a look at the pocket battleship *Aurora* that had been in action back in 1904–05, in the Russo-Japanese War. The red flag hung wearily from the mast. To me the ship seemed pretty small and ready for the scrap heap. Then a brief view of the Winter Palace, outside which the Bolshevik uprising or, if you like, putsch had taken place in November 1917, and the golden spire of the Admiralty building. There was no time for anything else.

But at some point or other, perhaps on the second day, there must have been a grand banquet. I remember that I was sitting next to a giant man wearing the magnificent uniform of an admiral of the Red Navy and sporting a large ring with a white cameo. To my question, he replied with a roar of laughter that it was a portrait of the Tsar Nicholas II, whom he much admired. By then the meal, with its countless toasts, had begun. And with the inevitable vodka glasses, filled to the brim. Sartre, who had the place of honour, seemed to be losing the fight with the alcohol. He had to admit defeat in the middle of the interminable succession of dishes that were being served. A discreet bodyguard conducted him to safety. Later, there was a rumour that a doctor had been called, but you don't have to believe every whisper you hear in the corridor.

On the last evening, things were more relaxed. It was, I think, Yevgeny Yevtushenko who saw to that. Three years younger than me, he knew exactly where to have a good time at night in Leningrad. The place he dragged us to was a kind of loft, the disused upper floor of a factory. There was a band that didn't just play waltzes and swing tunes but was also familiar with the latest fashions from the West. The *stilyagi* proudly showed off their leather jackets and genuine or imitation jeans. While the older generation got quietly but emphatically drunk, the younger crowd threw themselves into the twist until the early hours.

Only later did I discover how these lads kept up with the fashion—it was stations such as Radio Liberation and the Russian Service of the BBC, to which they owed their familiarity with the songs of Elvis Presley and The Beatles. They knew very well how to outsmart the Soviet radio jammers on the short-wave band.

The following evening we took the famous Red Arrow to Moscow. This sleeper train owed its reputation not least to lovers with nowhere to go, and who had little chance of finding happiness in their cramped flats. The twin-bed compartments were not only comfortable and cosy, because of the wide gauge, but also free from interruption, since they were allocated without regard to marital status. The journey took all of 10 hours, but no one complained about that.

In Moscow as well, the 'delegates' whom no one had delegated were immediately taken in hand. Our accommodation was in the Moskva, a hotel right on Red Square, opposite the Kremlin. Guests entered the box-shaped multi-storey building by a vast, poorly lit foyer with wide club chairs all round. In the corners, there were loudspeakers from which solemn choruses could be heard day and night. Groaning, overloaded lifts took the guests up to the ninth floor where a corpulent female monitor kept a record of our comings and goings and made sure no one went into the wrong room.

On the programme there was also an 'International Poetry Reading' held in a trade union building. It was so multilingual that the audience couldn't understand very much. More entertaining was a private invitation from Ilya Ehrenburg. His apartment in Gorky Street was so spacious that it reminded me of receptions given by people in Park Avenue or Rue de Varenne. On the walls were classics of modern art: a Matisse here and a Braque there or a Vlaminck. The champagne was served by maids in white caps, black blouses and embroidered lacy aprons. Canapés and petits fours were offered around. Our host's attempt to resurrect a long since vanished bourgeois age was remarkably convincing. I asked him, in French, about his stirring times in Paris where he'd been with Picasso, Modigliani, Apollinaire in Montparnasse, and Diego de Rivera at the Rotonde, and about his adventures in the Spanish Civil War. He was a man who had been through a lot, and had always fallen on his feet. I have to say that I liked him very much, better than Konstantin Simonov, who was also one of the guests. He looked as businesslike and efficient as the owner of a Swabian engineering works, very self-assured and very reserved. I happened to hear from someone else that over the weekend he'd flown in his private jet to his private hunting reserve in Siberia. There seemed to be more to Ehrenburg, for he had interesting ideas that he kept to himself as he pursued quite specific political goals.

The delegation had no opportunity to see any more of Moscow than the hotel, the Lenin Mausoleum outside the Kremlin or a 'People's Park of Our Achievements', for it was already time for a boat trip on the Moskva that took us as far as its confluence with the Oka, and lasted almost a whole day. To reach the pier and board the boat we had to go through a kind of station for ships, an imposing building—several stories high and crowned with a shining Soviet star. It was very warm. Since I didn't have a map, I had no idea where we were going. Clearly from here the capital was linked to far-distant seas, for there were not just pleasure steamers anchored at the quay but also freighters carrying their cargoes to the Baltic or the Caspian. The complex canal network of the Moskva and the Volga took us across large reservoirs and through huge locks adorned with columns that opened and closed automatically, as if by magic. We sat on deck under white awnings and enjoyed ourselves. Not only the Georgian wine but also the vodka flowed freely. I was amazed how well Hans Werner managed to keep up with the Russian writers whose table he was sharing.

Meanwhile, word of the real sensation of the day had gone around quickly. Nikita Khrushchev, the master of the gigantic country, had expressed his wish to talk to the writers gathered here, possibly even in his own house. Immediately the whispers started about who might be in on the visit.

As always, I couldn't hold my drink well enough and my Russian was too feeble for me to be able to join in the speculation. I was standing at the rail when a man, of about 40, spoke to me in English. He seemed to be interested in my opinion, as an outsider who was there for the first time, on the political situation in the country. I mentioned the much-discussed 'thaw', saying that for years it had been operated on a stop-go principle. The boss, I went on, had resolved to release the empire from its paralysis, to break up its entrenched attitudes, but that could only happen bit by bit, in phases—from one indigestible morsel to the next. For that reason no one could tell exactly where it was going to end and the result was an alternating cycle of hope and fear, not only among the intelligentsia but presumably everywhere else as well. He listened, amused as it seemed, and said that I wasn't entirely wrong there.

Later, my faithful guide Kostya whispered to me that the man I had been talking to was Alexei Adzhubei. Clueless as I was, the name meant nothing to me, and I was somewhat horrified when I learnt that I'd been talking so openly to Khrushchev's son-in-law and the editor of the government newspaper *Izvestia*.

There was another excursion on the programme, a day trip by bus to a place of pilgrimage: Tolstoy's house in Yasnaya Polyana. It's a mere 200 kilometres south of Moscow, that is, by Russian standards, quite close by. Everything there looks as if the master of the house has just left his study. His slippers are ready, the inkwell on his desk is full. I saw a 1910 newspaper lying there and a few letters that were addressed to him but he had presumably no longer been there to read them. Going around this carefully restored museum is like travelling back in time. It's so perfectly arranged that you hardly dare to admit the truth—what you're looking at is, of course, a touching fake.

Then, on 13 August, the day arrived. Early in the morning, I was at the airport with the other invited writers to take a special flight to Sochi. It was now clear who was on the mysterious guest list. Alongside the big names—Sholokhov, Tvardovsky, and Fedin, Sartre, de Beauvoir and Ungaretti—the instigator, the inevitable Vigorelli, was there. Among the locals there were a few worthy hacks from the time of the Great Patriotic War but otherwise notable authors were rather thin on the ground; instead, there were all sorts of chairmen and functionaries of associations from Russia, Bulgaria and Romania. Who was missing and why? Where were Ehrenburg and Yevtushenko? I started when I saw Alexei Adzhubei again, the son-in-law I'd chatted to in such an unguarded manner on the boat trip. And what had happened to Hans Werner? Why had he disappeared? I was afraid he might imagine I'd had something to do with it, but nothing was farther from my mind, for I'd have been happy to be able to hide behind him.

Then we were driven to Gagra, to Khrushchev's villa. I made notes about what took place there on 13 and 14 August 1963.

Our host comes through the door, slowly, taking short steps, using his arms for balance, an old man whose body is already giving him problems. His calmness is an expression of patience rather than anticipation of enjoyment. Hardly does he come to a halt, the ceremonies begin: introductions, handshakes, embraces. The effect is rather like amateur dramatics, but the direction is improvised: his smiles are not just standard grimaces, there's something ungainly about his gestures. The names and languages of his guests are foreign to him, even more foreign is their disposition. They're intellectuals, people full of mental reservations. He could well believe them capable of irony. The respect they show conceals reserve, arrogance, perhaps hostility. The visitors are a nuisance. They're pests.

He comes to meet them not without dignity. His peasant elegance isn't restricted to his embroidered shirt. It helps him get over many things. He can deal with the surreptitious mockery by quietly ignoring it. And his house, the park and the surroundings help too. These sophisticates are surveying everything with swift sidelong glances, giving the modern architecture a nod of approval, casting envious looks at the fragrant trees and the long, empty beach. The lord and master of it all feels a little spurt of pride. He demonstrates the glass wall which, driven by a concealed motor, opens out.

He manages with almost no bodyguards. The visitors aren't searched. His courage is attractive because he doesn't make a big thing of it. The rooms are too big for the man who inhabits them. He lacks the instinct for wealth. Small objects, which no architect included in the design, look out of place: a shabby little wall clock, an out-of-place pink ashtray. And the house is too tidy; it wouldn't miss its occupant and would be immediately available for any successor. Our host hadn't expressed any special wishes, hadn't chosen the wood himself. The furniture comes from the most expensive lines from the state factories. You see it in the hotel foyers in the capital, in the same colours.

We sit down in a small conference room. Our host doesn't present us with a programme, he hasn't prepared anything special. Chairs are shifted. For a few seconds no one seems to know what to do, then the guests make a start. They're no more confident than the man listening to them. They have been warned, it has been impressed upon them in private that the man they are to meet is not an educated person, so would they please take that into account: no foreign words, keep it simple; be careful and remember that your host, great even if short in stature, can be touchy.

All sorts of chairmen speak for three minutes each. Their thanks, their words of praise, their assurances are just a little too flowery, too unrestrained. He doesn't believe them. His hearing is precise. Sartre takes no risks with his few words; he adopts a wait-and-see, not to say meek-and-mild posture, quite in contrast to the way he behaves in France, where he likes to put on a show of courage involving no danger when faced with those in power. The only one to display a scrap of courage is the Pole, Jerzy Putrament. He demands more leeway for Soviet authors.

Even as the scene is played out, I have the feeling our host is more than a match for his guests. Weren't most of them, strangely excited, adjusting their ties, changing shirts, going over details of protocol again and again even while we were on the bus? Our host has no need for any of that. He's clear about his advantage.

That becomes apparent as soon as the writers' pious platitudes are over. Once more a moment of indecision. Then the first secretary of the Central Committee stands up, rather hesitantly, and starts to speak. Interpreters shift their chairs. He just wanted to say a few words, he says apologetically. At first, he seems unsure of himself. I imagine that he treats his own people quite differently, that more will be drunk and they'll shout at each other now and then.

What follows is a 50-minute speech lacking any kind of logical, discursive coherence whatsoever. He starts calmly, a little haltingly, gets worked up, drags in examples and anecdotes, speaks faster and comes to a sudden halt at an unforeseen turn of phrase. He seems surprised at what he's just said. He doesn't want to take it back but certainly isn't going to leave it as it is. He doesn't know how to go on, but don't worry, something will occur to him. Just be patient. Patience he has aplenty. He waits, hands clasped. It's the others who are nervous; they're afraid the speaker's got stuck. Thirty seconds. Then another sentence is there. It comes out of the blue, starts from a point no one had thought of. The connection will have to be worked out afterwards, or not at all, the associations lead us a merry chase. Absolute, disarming naivety? Only the more stupid ones in the audience have the feeling they know better. They're wrong, for hardly a single one of his apparently simple-minded statements is groundless; there's almost always something right, at times even enigmatic, about them. You don't get carried away by Khrushchev's speech; what there is about it that makes you think is his common sense and his shrewdness, his boldness and his nose for what is possible. In linguistic terms, he tends to reduce the unknown to the known. An even delivery, restricted vocabulary, minimal syntax. Rhetorical flourishes stick in his throat; they sound unconvincing, which the speaker immediately notices. Even his indignation doesn't seem fresh, it sounds as if it's occurred to him a hundred times before. He doesn't see why it should be necessary to keep on repeating things that are so obvious. He doesn't present many insights but he's sure of those he does. Doubts seldom surface, but for that very reason they're a threat to the one experiencing them.

That becomes clear when our host, for no apparent reason, starts talking about Hungary. None of the previous speakers has mentioned the Hungarian uprising of 1956. But still, there is Sartre sitting at the table who added nothing to the others' words of greeting but one brief, empty sentence. What we now get to hear is an attempted justification. It's presented in a longwinded and clumsy argument: 'If our intervention was a mistake, then I am the main one to bear the blame. But today, after seven years, anyone can see that it wasn't a mistake.'

He takes the bull by the horns, brings out differences of opinion instead of sweeping them under the carpet. I have the impression he's unhappy with his guests' caution, their eagerness to stay in line. Of course, those present want something from him: more leeway for Soviet authors, trips abroad, exhibitions, the chance to publish. And perhaps there's something he wants from us: support in the media for his concept of peaceful coexistence and his disarmament initiatives. Yet he doesn't hesitate to confront us with the darkest episode of his rule. The wound that is Hungary still hasn't healed. He brings something out into the open over which the dust refuses to settle. He seems to be trying to convince not just us but himself as well. Unlike Vigorelli, Ungaretti and Alexey Surkov, he doesn't butter us up, which presumably means he has more respect for us than we have for him.

That is the only part of his speech where you feel it means something to him personally. After a pause he abandons himself once more to his meandering associations, talks about anything and everything in a way that sounds almost muddled and gossipy. Later on, a couple of fairly senior officials tell me they are very concerned about his garrulousness. The boss, they say, is incapable of keeping a secret to himself, especially when it's a case of real or presumed success.

Quotations from his speech: 'We have abolished the dictatorship of the proletariat. After 45 years, we no longer need it. The Soviet Union is a people's state. Today we're a democracy. Only people who are afraid need a dictator.' He defends the idea of prosperity against the arguments of the Chinese: ' "The better off you become, the more bourgeois your way of thinking becomes," one of their delegates told me. But if a man buys himself a second pair of trousers, is he any the worse Marxist for that? I asked him whether he thought the best Marxists went around with no trousers on at all.' At times he boasts, carries on about the strengths of his country: 'It's not because the capitalists have become wiser but because we are now stronger that the Moscow agreement banning nuclear weapon tests was agreed. Without the Caribbean Crisis we might not have got the treaty.' He talks about more far-reaching agreements that Dean Rusk, the American secretary of state has come up with, offers that go far beyond what has been discussed in public. (There are rumours doing the rounds in Moscow suggesting that the USA has offered the Iron Curtain countries a comprehensive aid programme in the spirit of the Marshall Plan.)

All this interspersed with little lectures about the evils of capitalism. To hear him explaining socialism to a man like Sartre is disarming. He often read about suicides in the Western press, he says. But that wasn't a private matter! 'In our country such things are rare. We examine every case thoroughly, we search for those responsible and try to improve conditions.' Sartre listens to these analyses stony-faced.

The only literary reminiscence in Khrushchev's speech is characteristic. He recalls a story he read in a liberal periodical in 1910 or 1911. He's forgotten the author's name. (It could have been Christoph von Schmid.) An estate-owner is approached in the street by a beggar who asks him for a kopek. He searches through his pockets but can only find a 20-kopek coin that he gives to the poor man. Beside himself with joy, the beggar falls to his knees to thank him. 'How little,' the estate owner says to himself, 'this man needs to be happy. For me, on the other hand, it would take at least 20,000 roubles to make me feel such rapture.' Khrushchev shows his outrage at the difference between the two characters in the story which seems so significant to him that he quotes it even today. Or he asks whom a worker is working for under capitalism. An example could tell us that: A man takes a job building a wall but he doesn't have the right to know what it's for. It could even be the wall of a prison where he will be locked up one day . . . The parable does not achieve its edifying effect and it's too late that the speaker realizes the risks involved in talking about walls given the existence of the 'protective rampart' in Berlin.

He feels most comfortable with picture-book fables. On the subject of the personality cult, he's reminded of the elephant. If one came to his village when he was a child, everyone wanted to see it. So many people turned up and gathered round it that he, as a little boy, didn't get to see the animal. And that's what it was like with the cult of personality. At Stalin's funeral, 106 people died on Red Square. His own daughter only managed to save herself by crawling under a car. Today, on the other hand, when he walked across Red Square someone would nudge another and say, 'Look, there's Khrushchev going past.' The other would shrug his shoulders and reply. 'Oh I know him. Sometimes he's even seen someone spitting on the ground.'

It's quite simple things that he finds irritating and disturbing. For example, Kennedy's private fortune. Why do the workers vote for such a rich man? He thinks for a moment. Then he has a flash of inspiration: the capitalists win the elections because *you* help them. As he says that, he turns to his guests. A few of the writers start, others are taken aback. However, our host immediately reassures them by adding that present company is, of course, excepted. But it is still a heavy responsibility they bear. And this was the only section that was related to his guests' work. To my relief, he didn't waste a single word on literature and aesthetics.

Perhaps he overestimates the influence of the writing fraternity. Perhaps he has in mind how malleable and how venal they can be, even though it often suited the Soviet state. But what he's saying runs counter to traditional Marxist theory and ultimately inverts the proposition that social being determines consciousness. If his assertion were to appear in *Pravda*, it would a minor sensation. In this context it just sounds like the recognition of a political reality, expressed by a man whose sole knowledge of Marxism comes from the *Short Course on the History of the CPSU(B)*.

Then the speech simply stops because the speaker has the feeling that's enough and doesn't bother with a final flourish that would be easy to achieve by sticking on a few clichés about peace, progress and the future. The applause is polite but sparse. We get up and go out for a walk.

It's very hot and his guests are suffering in their dark suits. Our host invites us to go for a swim. He'd like to get into the water himself. His visitors haven't brought bathing costumes with them. Shock, horror! What does protocol say? Some are at a loss what to do, others don't feel like a swim. Can one take a dip in the nude, as the head of state suggests, and that in the presence of the author of *The Second Sex*? Most prefer to sit down on the steps, chatting cautiously, while our host disappears into one of the two bathing huts. Only Vigorelli, an unknown author and I feel like a swim. We get changed in the other hut where we find three pairs of oddly shabby bathing trunks laid out for our host and in his size. They come down to our knees. I have to hold mine up with both hands. The 10 minutes I spent in the Black Sea were possibly the only comfortable ones of the day, for our host and for us. Only the bodyguard in his boat, ever-ready to save his master, showed any concern about our well-being.

The dinner, which goes on for two hours, is served on the terrace. Before that we are given the opportunity to see round the house. It recalls a film set from the 1930s and 40s: pink covers in the bedroom, chairs in the palm-court style. The few speeches are banal and delivered without enthusiasm, but the cuisine is excellent. The conversation is almost entirely in Russian. The man next to me, Fedin, doesn't seem very keen to translate what the foreigners say for our host, who's sitting diagonally opposite. Only the small talk is passed on. I, the youngest at the table, wouldn't have had much to say anyway.

Germany is only mentioned once and that in an incidental remark. Our host says that from where we're sitting he can see as far as Prussia. On the other side of the bay Walter Ulbricht, the leader of the GDR, has his summer house. That's all, not another word about politics.

Khrushchev eats and drinks very little. I have the impression he's bored, but he's very attentive and assiduous about offering drinks, Georgian wine and mineral water that gives off a slight smell of sulphur.

We sit there like well-behaved little boys, regaling ourselves on the good things on offer. Tongues are not
loosened, no one gets merry, no jokes are made. Our
host suddenly looks tired, his eyes are half closed,
there's just a hint of suspicion on the alert—he's only
listening with half an ear.

After coffee, the Russian poet Aleksandr Tvardovsky brings off his great well-prepared coup. He
has a long career behind him. He became famous
during the Second World War with a poem about a
soldier, Vasily Tyorkin, that was not only popular but
was awarded a Stalin Prize. Under Khrushchev, he
was entrusted with the editorship of *Novy Mir* and
saw to it that *One Day in the Life of Ivan Denisovich*
(1962), the work of a completely unknown author
called Aleksandr Solzhenitsyn, appeared in it.

A heavyweight in this company, then.

He reads *The Remarkable Adventures of Private
Tyorkin in the Other World*, a sequel to his epic poem
of the 1940s. Under Stalin's rule there was no question
of the poem being published and even after the 'thaw'
the censors considered it too risky to print. They
suggested a 'revision' which the author declined.

The version he read shows what the problem
was, for in the other world the good soldier, who
reminds one of Schwejk, encounters exactly the same
conditions as in the Soviet Union. He looks in vain
for a place where he can rest and when he tries to
complain, he's told it's pointless because all the people

there were living contented, happy lives; the secret police made sure of that. Those whose behaviour was exemplary could look forward to a very special privilege: a holiday in the bourgeois hell.

This type of epic satirical poem is a traditional genre in Russian literature. In its stanza form and phrasing it recalls Heine's *Germany: A Winter's Tale* (1844). It is very similar in its effect as I could tell from the man sitting across the table. 'Lyrical' and witty verses alternate and the punch lines hit their target.

Of course, we foreigners couldn't understand what was at stake. But our host listened carefully and put up with it for a whole 50 minutes. Occasionally he seemed concerned, a few times close to irritation, he found the 'poetic passages' boring but he couldn't resist the jokes, roared with laughter a few times, remained silent for quite a while after the end of the reading, then said tersely, '*Chorosho.*'

For the Soviet writers this was the crucial result of the visit, a cleverly contrived successful manoeuvre. The departure was a replica of our arrival: clumsy embraces, perfunctory handshakes secret relief on both sides. Only the functionaries, disguised as writers, from the socialist countries, among them a particularly wishy-washy man from East Berlin, put on a show of solemnity.

After this encounter, there isn't much that's unclear about Khrushchev. He's a man who would never have come to power through a plebiscite or parliamentary elections. He doesn't stand out. And that's probably what saved him. His strength is that of a person who is determined to survive. That is how he managed to survive Stalinism and the power struggles after the Georgian's death. There is no doubt about his caution and his staying power. He has a greater ability to master situations than to set them up. Not a man for grand designs, difficult to convince, impervious to theoretical argumentation, he only learns through trial and error.

His merits can best be described in negative terms. He's fairly free of the megalomania and persecution complex of his predecessors. His basic convictions are so plain and simple that they don't determine his behaviour; on the contrary, his behaviour is a case-to-case interpretation of them. Within the limits of his commonplace assumptions, he's unsure of himself and therefore open to instruction. He has no inkling of what his greatest political achievement is. It lies in the demystification of power. A man with no secrets at the apex of power, that is rare throughout the world; in Russia, it's unheard of. He is totally lacking in 'charisma'. One's response in his company tends to be boredom and never the fascination that is so effective in a man such as de Gaulle. He doesn't only rebut the cult of personality ideologically, which wouldn't mean very much, but through his person. Anyone who finds that disappointing doesn't understand what is at stake. In the atomic age, any Napoleon acclaimed by the masses could take the risk of collective suicide. The shoe with which Khrushchev is supposed to have thumped his lectern in New York is harmless in comparison. You might yawn at his table, but you don't feel threatened.

A short flight took all of us who had been there back to Moscow. No one felt any desire to discuss what we'd seen. The important foreign guests were in a hurry to catch the earliest flights to Paris, Rome or Warsaw. My faithful guide Kostya picked me up from the hotel and treated me to a long evening with a few stalwart friends in his little apartment on Aeroportovskaya Street One, in a building that, like a beehive, houses the less important members of the writing fraternity. There was too much vodka for me to remember what people were talking, complaining and laughing about.

The next morning, it was 15 August, I was leaning back, relieved, in my seat in the SAS flight to Oslo. My first trip to the Soviet Union had been worthwhile.

Nikita Khrushchev died, a quiet pensioner, in his house in the country in 1971.

Hans Koch, mentioned earlier, committed suicide in 1986. He left no farewell letter that might have explained his reasons.

Aleksandr Trifonovich Tvardovsky was replaced as editor of *Novy Mir* after the fall of Khrushchev; he died, embittered, in his dacha in 1972.

Written after I returned home:

Bill of fare
(1963)

On a lazy afternoon today
I look into my house and see
through the open kitchen door
a milk-jug   an onion on a chopping board
a cat's bowl.
On the table there's a telegram.
I didn't read it.

In a museum in Amsterdam
I looked at an old picture and saw
through the open kitchen door
a milk-jug   a bread-basket
a cat's bowl.
On the table was a letter.
I didn't read it.

In a holiday house on the Moskva
a few weeks ago I saw
through the open kitchen door
a bread basket   an onion on a chopping board
a cat's bowl.
On the table was the newspaper.
I didn't read it.

Through the open kitchen door
I see spilt milk
Thirty years' wars
Tears on chopping boards
Anti-rocket rockets
Bread baskets
Class warfare.
Below on the left, right in the corner,
I see a cat's bowl.

SCRIBBLED DIARY NOTES FROM A TRIP AROUND THE SOVIET UNION AND ITS CONSEQUENCES

(1966)

27 August. From Oslo to Moscow via Stockholm on a hot summer's day.

At Sheremetyevo Airport, I'm met by my friend Kostya Bogatyrev whom I had got to know during my first journey to Russia three years ago. We were delighted to see each other again, back then we got on well right from the start.

Like many East Europeans, Tibor Déry, for example, he speaks excellent, old-fashioned German. My Russian is lamentable. It consists of a few hundred words and some rudimentary grammar; it's just about good enough to deal with a waiter.

So I'm completely dependent on Kostya. I discovered that his father is the celebrated ethnographer Petr Bogatyrev. He had gone to Prague with Roman Jakobson and returned to Moscow in 1939. In the course of the purges, he was banished from the university. He was only rehabilitated after Stalin's death. So my friend Kostya grew up in a typical Russian scholar's family. When he came home after two years in the gulag, he translated poems by Rilke whom he admires. He keeps his books in glass-fronted bookcases. In 1965, Kostya took part in an evening devoted to German literature in Moscow in which he read a few of my pieces, perhaps in the translation by Lev Ginzburg, who had planned to publish a whole book by me in Russian; all that's come of it so far, however, is a few poems in periodicals, in *Inostrannaya Literatura* or in *Novy Mir*, probably when Tvardovsky was the editor.

This time I have a room in the Peking, a hotel that occupies the top floors of a fantastic skyscraper from Stalin's days. These lodgings, already showing their age, are clearly reserved for guests of the government and the Party. I am allocated a suite. It consists of an enormous hall, resembling a gymnasium, that's empty apart from an out-of-tune concert grand, a bedroom and a huge bathroom with a cast-iron bath lacking a plug.

I suppose I will get an explanation for my unexpectedly high status from the Soviet Writers' Association that is situated in Povarskaya Street in the Arbat district. The building, a neo-classical town house surrounded by a private park, looks as if an aristocratic family had lived there. (Ignorant as I was, I didn't know that it had belonged to the Rostov family from *War and Peace*, a fact that is well known to every educated Russian. I would just have had to pay proper attention to a monument in the garden that shows Tolstoy sitting in a chair to realize whose legacy the Chairman of the Board of the Soviet Writers' Association had assumed here, since 1934.)

No one in the West has any idea of the political significance, the power and wealth of this institution. Membership is a matter of survival for any writer. Exclusion is a threat to one's whole social existence. The association is a censorship authority, travel agency, paymaster and welfare office, all in one. It decides whose holiday and foreign trips receive approval. As an author you turn to it when you need a train or air ticket, a fridge, a stay in a sanatorium or a clinic. Attached to the association is the so-called *Litfond* that deals with the administration, allocation and repair of apartments and dachas.

So that's where I've been invited—or summoned —this afternoon. An extremely unusual building! On the one hand there are little cubicles full of the clatter of the typewriters of bureaucracy and on the other spacious rooms with crystal chandeliers and heavy velvet drapes over the doors. In one there's even a plaster cast of the Venus de Milo standing around.

The visitor is offered brandy beneath the mild gaze of Gorky. The head of the commission for writers from Western countries—unfortunately, I've forgotten his name—has brought a specialist in German literature and a few minions with him. The only explanation I have for why he should put on such a show is that three years ago I was by chance, not to say, by mistake invited to Khrushchev's summer residence. But there is much to be said against this supposition, for the leader who entertained us in Gagra back then had been ousted a year ago. You couldn't accuse his successor, Leonid Brezhnev, of a profound interest in literature. Since then the political climate has felt frosty again and that has repercussions for writers. In 1964, Joseph Brodsky was arrested in Leningrad and condemned to five years forced labour for being a 'parasite'; he was released only recently because the case had sparked an international outcry. And he wasn't the only one. The same thing happened to Andrey Amalrik. And, Andrei Sinyavsky felt the consequences for having had his critical essays published abroad under the pseudonym, Abram Terz. In a Stalinist-type show trial at a Moscow court he was sentenced to seven years internment in a prison camp with hard labour. That all these scapegoats happened to be Jews cannot be due to mere chance. It recalls the campaign against 'rootless cosmopolitans', the ruler in the Kremlin unleashed at the beginning of the 1950s and the notorious doctors' conspiracy he invented shortly before his death. Many Soviet authors, artists and scientists immediately sensed a return to the conditions of Dzhugashvili's final years.

People such as Sakharov or Paustovsky refused to accept that. They sent an open letter of protest to Brezhnev. A new wave of dissidence spread across Russia. But not a syllable of this was to be heard in the house of the Writers' Association.

It was only later that I learnt that a meticulous record of all foreign scribblers is kept in this building and that there are specialists for every country and every language, who read everything these people publish. Not only books but also political remarks are noted down in the dossiers. A curriculum vitae is prepared and kept up to date; even newspaper cuttings and reviews are included in the files. I too have probably been classified in one of the precisely differentiated categories that determine how one fares here. Alongside the 'anti-Soviet' and 'reactionary' writers, there are also the 'progressive bourgeois writers'. They are treated particularly well, much better than foreign communists who, though pampered with large editions and generous royalties, tend to be regarded as useful idiots. All that suggests a belief in the political relevance of literature which seems pretty over the top.

Not only do they confirm my invitation to a 'Peace Congress' in Baku, they even propose a journey right across the Soviet Union 'so that I can get to know the country better'. And not in the usual form of a 'delegation', no, I'm being allowed to travel alone, with an interpreter. It's a privilege that's not granted to most visitors. I immediately suggest Kostya, whose excellent knowledge of German I wouldn't want to be without. After a brief consultation that is also approved and a plan is worked out for the trip that will last a month, taking me through the depths of the empire.

As I know from Russian novels, there were 13 grades in the tsarist civil service. And that has changed less than one would imagine. A little old man, perhaps of the fourth of fifth grade, beckons me over and presses a pretty fat envelope with rouble notes in my hand. And what is this money for? He's amazed at my question. But you're our guest, he says. Should the people we invite live on thin air? My objections are waved away. 'Just take it as an advance on your royalties from future publications.'

That evening in the neighbouring writers' club no expense is spared. There's even Sevruga caviar served in silver dishes. The building looks like a banker's or merchant's villa that was expropriated after the revolution. It is only open to registered members and their guests. I meet some of the people I saw in Leningrad again. Above all, the German scholar and translator Lev Ginzburg is there. He quotes Pasternak who said, 'The only characters in Shakespeare's plays who talk about morality are the criminals.' Perhaps he has some official members of the club in mind whose books no one reads but who have a nice apartment, a chauffeur and a house on the Crimea.

After a while, I notice that something seems missing in this city. Suddenly I realize that it's the neon advertisements, the company signs and trademarks. Instead of being pleased at their absence, I miss them, an indication of how conditioned by the commodities extravaganza our consciousness is. On the other hand, even in Moscow the number of cars in the streets has increased threefold over the last three years. Was that what Walter Ulbricht meant when he said they'd overtake the West instead of merely catching up with it?

The famous GUM on Red Square is so called because it is the 'State Universal Store'. It's been there since 1893. At that time it was the largest department store in Europe. The old Bolsheviks didn't like it. It was closed for a long time after the revolution. Its resurrection only came after Stalin's death and that was due to Khrushchev. With its fantastic labyrinth of staircases, corridors, glass cupolas, columns and galleries, it recalls Piranesi's *Carceri d'invenzione*. Sometimes you can buy things there that are unobtainable in other shops. That's why the departments of GUM throng with customers from the whole of the Soviet Union and no one complains about the long queues at the counters.

Moreover the fetish for brand names has no more withered away in Russia than the power of the state.

On the contrary, goods from the West count as status symbols here. As the lack of ordinary consumer goods diminishes, inequality increases. A Moscow woman I know has specialized in collecting Quelle and Neckermann mail-order catalogues and hiring them out by the week. She also has Burda patterns she hires out to private dressmakers. Anyone who is allowed to travel to the West is, of course, privileged. But people give them shopping lists and expect them to come back with the items. It can be some vital medicine but also a fashion accessory or a particular toy. This obligation causes problems for the traveller, who can't carry foreign currency out of the country, with the result that he has to beg from his hosts.

What is striking about the stations in Moscow is the presence of people from a hundred nations: Leningradsky, Jaroslavsky, Kazansky, Belorussky, Kievsky, Kursky—each station is a huge caravanserai. The waiting rooms recall wartime. The passengers bring their food with them and sleep on the floor. They have unlimited time. If you don't travel across the country, you can always undertake an expedition around the stations to get an idea of the babel of languages and costumes.

29 August. Departure for Baku to the 'Peace Congress' organized by the Writers' Association. It's seven in the morning. At the airport Kostya, Lev

Ginzburg, the novelist Vasily Aksyonov and a couple of others I don't know are sitting round a table in the departure lounge. All of them are well travelled. None of them talks about what's in *Izvestia*. Ideological statements are taboo at the breakfast table. Instead the passengers have brought their bottles of vodka. They're drinking from tumblers. *Sto gramm*— 100 millilitres—is the minimum measure. I can't keep up with that, which means an immediate loss of face in this company.

Ginzburg starts moaning about the Chinese. As I know, that expresses a widespread attitude in the Soviet Union. On this point many people are suddenly in agreement with the authorities that only a few years ago had locked them up and sent them to the gulag. It's not just because of the border conflicts which have been smouldering along the Amur and Ussuri rivers for years. Only recently Mao, the 'great helmsman', proclaimed the Great Proletarian Cultural Revolution, unleashed the Red Guards and called for the 'storming of the headquarters'. And by that he meant the Central Committee of the Party.

You in the West ought to be grateful to us, Lev and Kostya say, for we, the Russians, are protecting you from the 'yellow peril'. The fascination of the Western intelligentsia with China, they call snobbery. The two Russians compare Mao with Hitler: both had not only burnt books but also plunged their country into the abyss. And what about Dzhugashvili? I ask. Such comparisons arouse a certain unease, even among those who suffered under the purges; at least, the Red Army repelled the German invasion. One of them even tells me, in private, that the Americans know very well why they intervened in Vietnam otherwise the communists would eventually conquer the whole world. Thus, even in the early morning, positions can be reversed when the vodka flows.

In Baku there are flowers everywhere, flags, banners with the message that world peace is close to triumph. The hotel and the congress building: horrible concrete architecture. The delegations from Asia and Africa greet each other joyfully, clearly many of the delegates know each other from previous times.

Yevgeny Yevtushenko's also there. He's the star of the congress. Surrounded by photographers. For Soviet conditions there's something of Hollywood about his appearance. To my surprise, he immediately recalls our meeting in Leningrad. He even remembers our rock 'n' roll evening outside the official programme.

I have the misfortune to be compared to him in some newspapers— and it seems as if the reverse is also true. It's the cliché of the *angry young man*. Yet, a phenomenon such as Yevtushenko is only conceivable in Russia. You only have to listen to him, the way he recites his verse with the flowing, thunderous delivery of a professional. That's not something he'd invented, it's been a tradition since Mayakovsky at least, but it probably goes back to the nineteenth century, just as the role of representative he claims, as if he were speaking for the millions who don't have a voice of their own. Naturally, he arouses the envy of his rivals, who suspect him—and say so—of playing along with the government and writing to order. It is true that not everyone has the privilege of appearing on the front page of *Pravda* with, for example, a poem celebrating Yuri Gagarin. On the other hand he once published a poem that said, 'Don't let him out! Guard his grave so he won't come back!'—or something like that. It was Stalin he meant, as everyone understood.

I don't even recognize the names of most of the participants at the congress. There are hundreds of writers: Indians, Arabs, Africans, Indonesians, including many Party members and fellow travellers. The Chinese have clearly not been invited or have declined to come. A man by the name of Eduard Claudius has come from East Germany. Not pleasant company. But Abe Kobo from Japan is there; his novel *The Woman in the Dunes* is a masterpiece. He sits there, his little face screwed up in concentration, hesitates to take his jacket off and listens politely as Yevgeny lays his whole life bare. He tells us he'd always wanted to give a reading in the Sports Palace and finally succeeded that summer. He read a poem to an audience of 150,000 over a background of applause that was itself applauded. He claims that left him 'completely cold'. It disappointed him, he went on, since for him it meant saying farewell to his youth. His public weren't happy with him for giving up his shouting period.

He lists the authorities he has to deal with: the chairman of the Writers' Association, the Party secretary, the censor, the editor and the man who decides on the allocation of paper. He complains that an edition of only 200,000 copies was authorized for his last book. 'They're suppressing me, for there were 380,000 advance orders for my book!' Then he claims the solidarity among Russian writers is a sham: whenever anyone criticizes another, he's immediately said to have stabbed him in the back. In that way dogmatism cripples its opponents—it infects them.

He's tireless. He tells us about a hundred-year-old peasant who replied, when asked about justice, that you have to fight for it, with cunning, otherwise you'll be killed and that's unjust, but not with too much cunning, otherwise you'll just be fighting for yourself and you won't notice, for your cunning won't be up to that. The fight of justice, the peasant says, is justice itself. I wonder if Yevtushenko thought that up?

I have to admit that he impresses me with his generosity, his poses, the way he sees through poses, his vanity, his honesty, his gestures, his routine, his fight against routine, his endless torrent of words, his long hands, his confessions, his lies, his friendship, his love of risk, his training, which is like that of a tennis player, his coquetry, his table talk and his thefts. He is just as capable of boundless trust as of boundless flattery and making boundless demands on others, especially women. Ginzburg tells me he likes to show off his conquests. Every time he says this is the woman for ever and the next time it's another and almost every time he's married to them.

He has always been allowed to travel, wherever he wanted, to Havana just as much as to Chicago or Paris. There was always someone there who'd get fresh strawberries from Georgia for him on the black market, at 32 roubles a bowl, as much as a bus driver earns in a week.

He knows everyone here. In the bus, he points at someone and says: he was an interpreter in the concentration camp. This one here's a rent boy. Then he introduces me to his 'teacher': he was a footballer and had become a good poet. He took this friend's wife away from him. But he still drank with him, he claimed. Together they're trying to reconstruct a 1945 poem, 'The Hospital'. Another piece is about an old kulak woman sitting by the Volga waiting for her land and her cow to be given back to her. She throws fish that she breeds into the river. Yevgeny claims that he had a good catch there with a rod from Finland and flies from Thailand.

Lots of stories like that. A pensioner in a little summer shack stands out on the collective farm with his advice. No one listens to him. The assembly starts meeting behind his back. The pensioner notices this and cries out, 'Why am I not dead?' And he starts to write poems—he who has spent his life making things difficult for all those who could read or write.

Compared with these anecdotes, the after-dinner speeches at the congress are indescribably long-winded. Foot-stomping fake folklore and ungainly female dancers, yelling poets. Yevtushenko calls the whole business a farce and refuses to read from his works. Then why did he bother to come at all?

In the middle of all this racket he manages to listen to a little 25-year-old man from Guatamala who has been living in Moscow for five years. The man is earnest, unhappy, fanatical and drunk. He considers himself a victim of colonialism and keeps going on at Yevgeny, whom he calls a kept playboy. The star embodies everything that little Roberto, who believes he's the great Obregón, has lost or never possessed. At no point does the Russian lose his self-control and clinks glasses with the sozzled poet. But all the others just carry on moaning.

The word *mat* keeps cropping up and I guess that it has something to do with mother. I ask Lev Ginzburg who roars with laughter. 'When you

Germans swear, it's always *Scheisskerl* and *Arschloch*. Here in Russia we prefer other obscenities. There's fucking every which way and your mum's not spared either.' That makes sense, just as *le con* and *le foutre*, slip easily off a Frenchman's tongue and a favourite American swearword is 'motherfucker'. Lev is definitely the right interpreter for words that aren't in the dictionary. 'You just be careful you don't confuse *mat*, *blat* and *bljad'*, they're very important words here. *Bljad'* just means "whore" but you mustn't take it literally. *Blat*, on the other hand, means everything that goes on behind the scenes, illegally or, if you like, by corruption, most things, that is.'—'In Germany, we used to call that *to organize* something or *Vitamin C*, "C" for connections.'—'Well there's no other way. So, please make a note of that.'

The next day, I listen as one of the censors chats Yevgeny up. Personally, he says, he admires him, of course, and loves his poems. 'A man who loved the birds died. A flock of birds flew round his grave. But who will come to my grave? My work is dirty. Where is the cage, Yevgeny? It's precisely the passages I have to cut that I love. But others might misunderstand and use them against us. What can a single person do, against so many?'—He too has obviously had too much to drink and is wallowing in self-pity.

I prefer to have a discussion with Raymond Kunene, a Zulu from South Africa with an English and an Ethiopian passport. I ask him how long apartheid will continue. He says things are starting to turn against the whites; the atom bomb won't help them at all. Their secret sense of insecurity, their fear; sooner or later the regime must collapse. Does he know that no one in the world will intervene? 'That's a matter of course. Look at Vietnam! The Chinese are right, he goes on, when they say that, just like the FLN and all the other liberation movements, the Vietcong have to win by their own efforts.'—'That sounds cynical.'—'But it's true. We're preparing for guerrilla warfare.'—'So you'll kill three million people? No. Some whites will go of their own accord, not just some of the worst but some of the best as well. We'll make peace with the rest, as in Kenya.'— 'But you'll hate them so much you won't be able to live together with them!'—'Why not?' Once you're victorious, he says, the enemy deserves respect rather than hatred.

The professional peaceniks make very long, empty speeches, identical in 15 languages. They can't mention Vietnam without using the word *heroic*. The American war they call 'the death throes of Imperialism'. An intelligent Algerian, whose private conversation is acute and emphatic, joins in the chorus when he mounts the podium. I ask him why. He's not speaking for himself here, he replies, he's only been invited for the sake of appearances. His task is to deliver the communiqué of the boss he's representing. That, he concludes is *la règle du jeu*—the rules of the game.

I decide not to say anything at all on the podium. I just don't feel like taking up the fight against these windbags.

One comfort is the arrival of Margarita Aliger, a Jewish poet, around 50, whose dignity is matched by her knowledge of human nature and sense of humour. I was at her table during dinner. She obviously has no problem seeing through the postures that are usual here. Her reaction to the speeches at the conference hall is to look to high heaven in resignation.

I was introduced not only to her but also to her daughter, Masha. So then why is her name not Aliger but Maria Alexandrovna Makarova? She's 23 and studying American literature. Large eyes with a shimmer of green, a piercing, adult look and a child's hands. She trembles slightly as she eats and, like a rabbit, she's satisfied with a few lettuce leaves. She speaks a little French and Spanish but, above all, a pure, hesitant English that sounds as if she's learnt it from records.

In a dictatorship, public discourse usually consists of propaganda and the media must be approached with great caution. Only those familiar with the rules of the game can get usable information from it now and then. I remember the training that conditions during the Second World War gave me in this respect. And just as back then in Germany, here too this concealment of the facts is compensated by an unofficial news service: rumour, the grapevine. The more rigorously things are kept secret, the more unrestrained the gossip. You just have to ask the right people if you don't want to remain completely trapped in your own unawareness.

I was curious enough to ask around, and not only because I wanted to know more about Masha; I'd also been very impressed by her mother, who was sitting next to me at dinner. As usual, Kostya and Lev knew all about her and I learnt that Margarita Aliger had had a difficult and adventurous life. She was born in Odessa in 1915. Her name was partly an anagram, for her parents were called Seliger. Her life recalls the kind of story Isaac Babel wrote. As a young girl she went through the civil war in Odessa, with all the upheavals you can read about in Konstantin Paustovsky and Vladimir Jabotinsky. She was probably an ardent Bolshevik. At that time politics still gave hope. Everything was happening at once and most found it intoxicating: the key role of the intelligentsia, the opportunities for advancement, art, literature and the new cinema.

Her first husband was Konstantin Makarov-Rakitin. A child they had died at the age of one, in

1938. Makarov, whose surname Masha bears, fell in the war in 1941. During the war Margarita lived in Leningrad while it was besieged and the daily ration of bread was less than that in Buchenwald concentration camp. There she wrote a patriotic poem that all Soviet schoolchildren know; its heroine is a 12-year-old partisan called Soya who is shot by the Germans. Margarita was awarded the Stalin Prize for it; that and her Jewish origins were probably the only things she had in common with Ehrenburg. That prize, Kostya said, protected her for decades, even though she went around with the wrong sort of people; her friends included Anna Akhmatova and many others who were victims of the purges or only escaped them by the skin of their teeth.

Later, she was said to have married this Konstantin Makarov, a composer. That, Kostya says, would explain Masha's surname, although at the time her mother had a liaison with Alexander Fadeyev. His brief hour of fame came from his 1927 novel, *The Nineteen*. I knew it. The author was not untalented. Perhaps, he could have become a writer. His second book, *The Young Guard*, was already a hackneyed tome faithful to the Party line. Then he became a rabid Stalinist who controlled literary life in the Soviet Union for decades. That he once called Sartre 'a hyena at the typewriter' is the least of his sins. Sartre was in Paris where no Fadeyev could harm him. Unlike his

Russian friends, comrades and colleagues, whom he helped send to the gulag.

He appears to have never concerned himself with his daughter Masha. But I suspect she inherited the Tartar colour of her eyes from him: a radiant blue that has now a shimmer of metallic grey, now of turquoise.

What is certain, though, is that Fadeyev was a serious alcoholic and, after Khrushchev's famous speech in which he publicly denounced Dzhugashvili's crimes, he shot himself in his dacha in Peredelkino. He is reputed to have sent his farewell letter not to his wife or to his children but to the politburo. Even in Russia no one can understand what was going on inside a man like that.

I have neither the desire nor the intention to encroach further on Margarita's family secrets. I don't know whether to believe everything I was told in Baku or not. It is said that today she still has good connections that reach even as far as the Central Committee of the Party. Apparently, there is a third husband called Igor who is a member of that institution. Finally a journalist even whispers to me that Masha is unhappily married. In a country where there's no popular press, scandalmongering is rampant and mostly no more to be believed than *Pravda*.

What has struck me about the Soviet Union is the liberal attitude to relations between men and women.

You get married now and then, now and then you get divorced. There is no stigma attached to illegitimacy and, from what I hear, abortion is looked on as a standard form of birth control. Emancipation bears fruit that is beyond the wildest dreams of the women's movement in the West. I think it is connected with the burdens women have had to bear here, not just during the war but also in peacetime—in industry, on the collective farms, while their men were arrested, fell in battle or abandoned themselves to vodka.

Since she's obviously bored, I suggest to Masha that we escape from the congress circus and take a walk around the town. It's an unusually hot September day. There is ice cream and kvass on every street corner but Masha knows her way around, and we sit down in a café on the boulevard along the beach. So there you have a Russian and a German in Azerbaijan talking to each other in English. Architecturally, the town presents a hotchpotch of art nouveau, Gothic revival and Soviet architecture. Masha explains that the richest houses go back to the oil boom that started as early as the end of the nineteenth century. Alfred Nobel's brothers were some of the first entrepreneurs who made immense fortunes; the Rothschilds were involved as well. The wind coming off the Caspian Sea smells of petroleum. It's only in the old town that Islam is still alive. There's also a real oriental bazaar where we spend a lot of time wandering around.

A funfair has spread itself out on the high hill at the back of the town; it has an illuminated big wheel you can see for miles around and we can't resist it. There's also a restaurant with a facade of columns nearby. Inside, the approach to dress is democratic— everything goes, from a long gown to a threadbare jacket. The chandeliers cast their light on red carpets where hungry cats search for scraps. In the darkness, it comes to a tête-à-tête in the grass. That was the beginning of an *amour fou* that has all the makings of a tempestuous Russian novel.

The next day there's an excursion to Neftanye Kamni. Along with Kostya, there's Marina Pavchin-skaya, a young interpreter who speaks very good German. She's already been on a visit to the Federal Republic once. To my surprise, she says, 'I was disappointed by the lack of individuality in your country.'

The first thing I see when the ship ties up is a corrugated iron shack. Marina translates for me what someone's written on the wall. It says, *La dolce vita*. The whole place consists of posts and planks with perforated cement slabs laid over them. The foundations are slowly rusting through. There's a rumble of thunder from the planks under the wheels of our open cars. It all recalls 1919: everywhere there's an echo of history, like the constant clatter of the electric carts transporting chunks of rock.

The plank-town stretches out for miles and miles. It's surrounded by an archipelago of islands: oil platforms and derricks. The Caspian Sea is unpredictable, within a couple of hours the wind can turn into a violent storm. The hazards are the cliffs and sunken wrecks. Brown patches on the surface of the water, a scurf of tar on the bizarrely hollowed-out rocks. The first wells that were sunk incurred heavy losses, there were constant accidents. Now there are brick-built houses, a restaurant and an open-air cinema. The fantastic silhouette hovers over the horizon. A black, industrial Venice brought alive by seagulls and cats. Everything looks as if it's crumbling, patched-up, cobbled together out of leftovers. Nothing of the cold-blooded, calculated superiority of the Americans, whose approach to nature is that of technological masters.

The workers with their heavy, savage faces seem self-assured—as if they really did belong to a 'ruling class' as the textbooks maintain. There's still something of the heroic determination of the early years about this forcible industrialization. The view recalls the sooty, grainy texture of early Eisenstein films. The generators and drills don't belong to the electronic age in which even petrol engines are now starting to look archaic. This is the way the first mining settlements in Spitzbergen must have looked, the way science-fiction writers imagine the first primitive colonies on other planets.

Everywhere in the Soviet Union visitors are taken around exhibitions with machines and industrial products, 'culture parks', collective farms and 'peoples' palaces', and that was the case in the Azerbaijan Socialist Republic as well. Foreign tourists, who have seen better architecture, find the monotonous high-rise buildings of preformed concrete slabs depressing. Heads of Marx formed with flowers, mass-produced statues of Lenin, the plaster cast art of the memorials —they find it all both moving and tedious.

In Baku there was also the opportunity to chat with Russian millionaires such as Roman Karmen, the documentary film-maker who made *The Nuremberg Trials*, about the tribunal where former Nazis were judged in 1945–46; or Konstantin Simonov, a reporter and mediocre novelist who fell out of favour with Khrushchev because of his 1953 hymn to Stalin, but can now pursue his career as a political journalist again. They are old, melancholy war-horses, well-travelled men who, like Hemingway, have seen many wars, in Spain, in the Far East, in Cuba or in Vietnam. Their reports are studied in the military academies. They are notable for a certain serene cynicism. They have come to terms with their privileges just as they have with their defeats.

Karmen talks about the capitulation of Japan and about his conversations with Mao. As far as the

Chinese are concerned, he limits himself to a quotation from Strindberg: 'It's a pity about the people.'

Finally, Kostya takes me to see a friend who works as a structural engineer in the building industry. A man with the grace of a bear. He sees himself as the builder of Baku. The city is full of 'his' schools and houses. His wife comes from Ossetia—a Caucasian profile, jet-black hair, black eyes, a long, curved nose. No beauty, but proud and sweet-tempered.

The dinner is sumptuous, the best I've eaten so far on this journey. Our host talks dismissively about the police, who can't do much with the mountain folk who speak a hundred different languages that vary from village to village. And the Party is frustrated by their archaic customs. There are people over a hundred years old who have never seen a fish; there are only pack-horse tracks, no roads, no tobacco, no newspapers, no alcohol, no telephones. According to standard Islamic practice, the women are workhorses and don't take part in conversation. These are islands, the last remnants of a broken ark. No one, our host says, can convert these people to communism, it's impossible to break them, and to bend them would take a hundred years.

He's interested in the West, that he doesn't know, but he's neither hypnotized by our way of life nor does he criticize it. Instead, he asks about wages and rents. He puts aside prejudices with a laugh. When Kostya's interpreter's skills fail, he resorts to mime.

After the meal, we watch TV. By chance it happens that a reading is being broadcast. And, of all people it's Yevtushenko. He doesn't go down well here. His exhibitionistic side is dismissed with a shrug. The poet here encounters the kind of critic Brecht wished for, but seldom found. This viewer makes distinctions effortlessly, and fairly ruthlessly at that. Then, without further ado, he goes back to being our host and pours us Georgian brandy.

On the last evening in Baku, the congress has finally run out of steam. We're both impatient to get away. What I'd most like to do would be to go off with Masha to Peredelkino, where her mother has a dacha in the woods, and leave all these questions of politics behind. But that's out of the question. It's my own fault. Why did I agree to go on this long journey of discovery that is going to take me as far as Siberia? We'll write to each other, looking forward to the day when we can see each other again in Moscow.

3 September. By plane with Kostya to Tashkent via Ashgabat. We are among the privileged, we board first and are seated in an upholstered compartment. As always the cabin is stuffy and the food, distributed by the adipose stewardess, pretty inedible. While the plane is changed, we break the journey close to the airport. So that was the desert, that was Asia; the only noise the chirping of the crickets. Beside the sandy track, an old woman is selling honeydew melons to thirsty travellers. Never has the fruit tasted better.

In Tashkent we are picked up from the airport by people from the Writers' Association as usual. The streets a teeming throng of tribes and languages. Clothing, manners and body language change from one corner to the next.

Five months ago the clock of the tower on Revolution Square, a landmark of the town, stopped. The epicentre of the earthquake was eight kilometres down, precisely below the city. Astonishingly, in the city of a million inhabitants only 15 people died. More than 30,000 houses, mostly built of clay, were damaged or destroyed. The concrete and masonry buildings withstood the earthquake. The ruins in the centre of the town have already been levelled. Workers and machines, whole construction combines, were called in from all parts of the Soviet Union. The tents, where they were housed, can still be seen. They made a real effort, quite different from Turkey where a similar earthquake has just claimed three thousand victims. There the homeless, it is said, are still sleeping on the bare ground.

The forcible establishment of the *Pax Sovietica* with its prison camps has ensured that in Central Asia the multinational state has survived without civil war.

Lenin's policy regarding nationalities claimed many victims, but also put an end to blood feuds that had gone on for centuries. I wonder whether, from an economic point of view, the Soviet empire has actually been worthwhile. A university was established somewhere among cotton fields and camels—what do the Russians get out of that, when all's said and done? Even during tsarist times the expense was probably much greater than the return.

5 September. I travel to Bokhara with Kostya. The town seems grey, lifeless, grubby and morose, as if time had passed it by. There is no trace of the glory of the Silk Road in the bazaar. Most of the customers go barefoot, only the Russians are wearing shoes. The vendors sit on the ground in front of their wares. Outside a little inn the customers are sitting cross-legged in the open or stretched out on mattresses, as if they were having a siesta. Beyond a slum quarter are the high-rise buildings made of preformed concrete slabs with the same shops and empty department store as everywhere else. There are no package tourists here, but we're still shown everything that can be regarded as worth seeing: mosques, madrassas, Orthodox churches.

There is little to remind you that the city was once a great centre of science. Not even the most celebrated son of Bokhara, the universal scholar Ibn Sina or Avicenna, has made it to a memorial here. In the summer residence of the emir, who is said to have fathered 500 sons, there's a large, stone-rimmed basin. It is said that from his throne at the top of the steps the ruler would select those of the daughters of his country who were to bathe there. Apparently, he would throw a golden apple to the chosen one of the day. Her clan would have nothing against that, for the emir's wish was regarded as an honour and the young woman's future was secure in the harem.

6 September. Our journey continues without a pause for breath. The next stage is Samarkand, nowadays in Uzbekistan. Pleasant temperatures. A medley of languages: Russian, Uzbek, Kazakh, Farsi, Turkmen, Kirghiz . . . Even the Pashtuns of Afghanistan aren't that far away.

In its splendour the city recalls Isfahan. True, here too the concrete mania of the planners has largely defaced the townscape, but what has remained—the blue mosques, the Koran schools, the palaces and the 'academies'—are marvels of the centuries-old Islamic civilization. Omar Khayyam, the famous Persian author of the Rubaiyat, mathematician and astronomer, is said to have pursued research and written poetry here. I can only vaguely remember what he did with cubic equations and binomial coefficients. And, I'm still disturbed by these stupid problems of transcription: Should it be Hayyam, or Khaiiyam, Rubaijat or Rubaiyyát?

Some way outside the city we go around the ruins of the observatory of Ulugh Beg. He was a prince, grandson of Tamerlane. Astronomy was his passion. The fifteenth-century observatory was a round, three-storey brick edifice that was destroyed after he was murdered. Russian archaeologists disinterred the remains before the First World War.

Together with the scientists he recruited from Persia, Ulugh Beg calculated the inclination of the ecliptic, the precession of the equinoxes and, with a precision unmatched in his day, the length of the sidereal year. Since there were no effective telescopes in his day, he had to use a large sextant for that. The subterranean part of that instrument, that had a diameter of 36 metres, can still be seen today.

These researchers' calculations and methods are also still extant: tables of the trigonometric functions, the beginnings of an astronomical almanac, astrological data and, above all, a catalogue of stars giving the positions of a thousand heavenly bodies with astonishing precision. There's something sublime about this Islamic research. A guide, who explained all this to us, quoted a scholar, I've forgotten his name, who said, 'Happy the man who leaves the world before it has no more need of him.'

The next day there's an excursion out into the hinterland. A young Uzbek called Andrei has persuaded his father, a teacher with strict beliefs, to invite us. We are entertained in oriental fashion. A wether has been slaughtered. We are given local wine. The elevated language of the toasts: 'Regard this house as your own.' Preserved tomatoes, grapes, melons, plums from their own garden. There's also a large bed there, more of a divan for the siesta of the woman of the house who suffers from a heart condition. Their daughters are supervised and guarded so that they're not in danger of losing their virginity. Andrei, who longs in vain for a car, is not allowed to smoke in his father's presence; only on the way back does he light up one Troika after another.

That evening there's an announcement on the radio that doesn't sadden any of us: Hendrik Verwoerd, the architect of apartheid, has died in Cape Town with a knife in his belly.

8 September. We fly to Alma-Ata, the Kazakh capital. The city is in very good condition. The peak of Talgar, over 5,000 metres high, can be seen from everywhere in the centre. The setting in the landscape with the snow-covered Altai Mountains and their glaciers is spectacular. It isn't very far from Alma-Ata to the Chinese border—you have to get used to quite different geographical coordinates here. Stretching away to the north are the steppes. A liberal supply of parks and gardens. Apricots, melons, tobacco and vines. The climate is mild, only at night does it get cool.

As usual, I immediately asked Kostya where the station is. Since the 1930s Alma-Ata has been an important station on the Turksib railway. Even before the war Stalin saw to it that there was a magnificent station. Our hosts, among them a translator of Goethe, a writer of comedies and a professional peace lady, insisted on showing us the large Orthodox cathedral. It's the tsarist wedding-cake style, made of wood and has clearly never burnt down.

What is striking is an interest in Europe that is close to yearning. We were taken to the bookshop on the corner of Sogolya and Seifulina that specializes in German literature: Schiller, Goethe, Heine sitting cosily beside authors from East Germany, Volker Braun, the Leipzig Insel Verlag, handbooks of medicine and botany. I'm told that after 1933, a large number of German émigrés lived here. That would be a good research topic in itself (fleeing, settling in another country, the purges, the gulag, rehabilitation, etc.). Why don't you spend a week here? Can't you get more translated from Kazakh? It's difficult to disappoint all this belief.

Absurdly, we dine in a Finnish restaurant that evening. How has the owner managed to end up here? When you're invited out like this the table never fails to be decorated with a bouquet of little paper flags and there's always an American one among them. Perhaps, that's a gesture of the 'peaceful coexistence' Khrushchev liked talking about so much.

By now we've stumbled at top speed through Bokhara, Samarkand and Alma-Ata. There's something crazy about this journey. It's impossible to keep up with it in my notes. One reason is the solicitude, control and rituals of our local hosts who stick to their instructions. In the evenings, after the inevitable dinner parties, toasts and lengthy drinking sessions, during which I manage to pour out most under the table, Kostya and I sit together in the hotel room and work out the reports about me that my friend, who has to work for the KGB of course, must deliver: praise for the 'achievements' and critical remarks in the right measure.

9 September. An intermediate stop in Novosibirsk. During the flight the Altai Mountains in the east. Over west Siberia small clumps of trees can be made out in the grey of the steppes. The water table is high, a lot of marshland. Later the dense coniferous forest of the taiga. Then the mighty Ob, shallow and sluggish as it branches out into an estuary with large green islands.

I'm glad to be back in the north again. Kostya says goodbye here. Marina Pavchinskaya is to take over from him; she was at the congress in Baku and from now on will accompany me as interpreter and KGB informant. She's less confiding than my friend, but quick-witted and intelligent. The airport is casual, evidence of the self-assurance of the nearby city of over a million people. In its relaxed ambiance it recalls American conditions.

After two hours we fly on. The immense sky of Siberia. The ecological and climatic changes can be observed with the naked eye. Drowned trees everywhere.

During the flight a conversation with Marina about the 'system'. She sees the contradiction between the councils (i.e. 'soviets') and the Party, mentions the 1921 Kronstadt rebellion of sailors and workers that was put down with much bloodshed by Trotsky. She has problems with her own role as an informant. Always these delegations she has to take around!

10 September. Arrival in Irkutsk. With my very first breath I can sense the smell of the taiga, mixed with the fumes of industry. Irkutsk, a settlement founded 300 years ago, is the largest town in the region. Its character is pure Russian even though you can see a lot of Buryat or Mongolian faces. In the centre there are stucco palaces from the tsarist period, theatres like little offshoots of the Petersburg models, blockhouses with tarred planks on the roof, beautifully carved tracery on the painted shutters.

The city lies on the Angara and on the Trans-Siberian Railway that goes as far as Vladivostok and via Ulan Bator to Peking. The conquest of such vast territories the recalls the heroic period of the American West, the impulse the railways barons gave to the expansion of the American empire, the one difference being that there the thrust was westward rather than eastward. The military strategists and men looking for raw materials always knew the value of such uninhabited areas that were thus conquered. You find a different kind of geography here: China and Central Asia, America and Japan are closer than Europe.

Was the course of the Trans-Siberian Railway planned so that it took in the towns situated on the large rivers, or was it the other way round, and the towns owe their existence to the railway? Irkutsk was certainly there before the railway. Even during the time of the tsars, it played an important role, not only in consolidating their rule over Siberia but also for those who had been banished there, for the convicts and for forced labourers who were sent there to build the railway.

The most celebrated deportees were the Decembrists. There are two museums devoted to them, housed in the old palaces of Prince Volkonsky and Prince Troubetzkoy. In the old days, many a conspiracy was hatched in these carefully reconstructed wooden buildings. Handcuffs, shackles, court documents and letters are on display, but also embroidery by the women and a cembalo for noble lords who were under house arrest. Bakunin, who was banished to Siberia for life, also spent a few years here. He is said, as we are told, to have been related to the governor and was well treated until he managed to escape to Europe via Japan and California. Later it was the gulag prisoners who came, the refugees and the prisoners of war who suffered worse treatment than those persecuted during the time of the tsars. There is a whole wall devoted to photos of 'the graves of our brothers', the Russian name for the fields where many unknown prisoners were buried.

We are also shown the tomb of Grigory Shelikhov, who in the eighteenth century colonized the Aleutian Islands for the tsar and explored Alaska. He is known as 'the Russian Columbus who found unknown lands.' You have the feeling that even today the loss of Alaska, that Tsar Alexander II sold to the USA, causes the Siberians a kind of phantom pain.

A few hundred yards further on the modern town, with its desolate apartment blocks, colleges, government offices and 'combines'—as the large industrial concerns are called throughout Eastern Europe—spreads like a tumour, far out into the surrounding countryside.

Despite the immense remoteness, the feeling that Russia is culturally part of Europe is still alive. I notice that not only in the conversations with writers and professors but also in the young people. I was invited to a celebration at a school, where I had to cut the red ribbon in a gymnasium to open a new 'club'. The faces of the teachers—limited but willing. As in all schools, there was a smell of subjection there but the girls were lively and stunningly naive. One of the girls in the youth organization, Komsomol, who had learnt French and longed to go to Paris shouted, *'J'aime les hommes.'*

Although at this time of the year there's no question of 'Siberian cold'—in the middle of the day the temperature reaches 15 degrees—in our hotel, the Siberia, there's a filled hot-water bottle and a Bakelite thermos flask for the tea. A local saying is, 'A hundred millilitres is no vodka, a hundred roubles no money, a hundred kilometres no distance and a hundred years no age.'

I try to ring Masha in far-off Moscow as often as possible. Three hours time difference—is that the reason why I get no answer, or has she chosen to live out at the dacha, where there are often problems with the telephone? I decide to confide in Marina. She advises me to keep my impatience in check and to beware of the bureaucratic traps one has to reckon with in this society, even in places where a foreigner wouldn't expect them.

11 September. The very next day we fly to Bratsk. The airfield has a temporary look. Little single-engine biplanes and high-winged monoplanes. Without them most places in the north would be inaccessible. The building, thronged with passengers, has no waiting rooms. I'm told the low, dirty, dilapidated old shack is to be pulled down soon.

Why Bratsk? Why was this out-of-the-way place included in the itinerary? Why is it a compulsory stop on the schedule for foreign visitors?

The reason is the labour of Hercules that has been carried out here. It can be seen in an ocean at the confluence of the Angara and the Oka that was not discovered by Magellan or Cook but dammed up. The taiga has been torn up and turned into an immense building site. In 1952 it was decided in Moscow to dump Bratsk, a small seventeenth-century settlement, in the valley and drown it in a reservoir: a Vineta of the industrial revolution. That is to be understood literally, for extreme force was used in the construction of the dam and hydroelectric power station. It was nothing new here. In 1947 there was already a penal camp here in which 50,000 prisoners were used as forced labour to build the railway line from Lake Baikal to the Amur River.

We're shown the 5,000-square-kilometre reservoir and the mile-long dams. To construct them, they had to set up a concrete factory that is still in operation. We're also taken to an aluminium smelting plant. I hold my nose. You don't need a gauge to see how all this industrial plant is polluting the surrounding area with dust and exhaust fumes.

But the real pride of the helpful souls who accompany us from the very start—are they specialists in industrial processes or in propaganda?—is naturally the centrepiece of all these efforts, the Bratsk hydroelectric power station. It's already two-thirds completed. Pylons with aggressive flashing lights carry the 500-volt lines to near and distant consumers. When it's completed it should have a capacity of generating 4.5 gigawatt. The ground beneath our feet is quivering. We're taken along deserted ferroconcrete pump galleries and can feel the turbines working in their casing.

As we're leaving the power station two hours later, I see a worker sitting in his cubbyhole. I noticed him when we went in because he seemed to be doing nothing, just dozing. I ask one of the engineers what's up with him. 'Oh him! He's been sitting in there for a few months now.'—'Is he ill?'—'No. Since his wife ran off he's been heartbroken. We try to talk him out of it, but it's best if we leave him in peace.' A brutal adherence to production targets and considerate tolerance, it's difficult to understand how the two can go together. In the control centre too, where a bored girl sits staring at the monitors, the work ethic is kept within limits.

Back in the new town, where the population has grown to 140,000 in 10 years. It consists of dreary, uniform apartment blocks in rigidly rectangular arrangements that are shown to us with pride. A room with heating, a bed and airtight windows—that is what is regarded as an achievement of communism here. I ask one of our guides what would happen if someone should have the idea of building a house of his own, after all there's plenty of room in the taiga. He gives me a baffled look and says, 'What would be the point? The plan sees to everything.'

There are still a few old wooden buildings left over from the time the town was founded. They are suited to the environment and the climate; like the old buildings decorated with carving in Irkutsk, they show the sure taste of the carpenters. As our guide, a supposed writer, probably an official, tells me, they are to be 'liquidated' as soon as possible.

The architect who planned these apartment blocks ought to be thrown in the Angara—if he exists. But the whole lot was probably designed centrally in

a Moscow ministry, a crime against architecture committed by some desk-bound bureaucrat who has
never been to the place. Or, was he the one who had
the cheek to cut the red tape with the Soviet star?

I hope that later these cages for humans will
be treated in the same way as their predecessors: liquidated in their turn, that is, assuming they haven't
collapsed beforehand. Like the old houses, Marina
and I are probably regarded as 'remnants of the past'
by the ruling technocrats. We agree that it would be
a good idea to provide the engineers of landscapes
and souls with a minimum of historical awareness.
But I fear that such an offer would fall on deaf ears.

The next morning a long conversation with the man
who constructed the power station. Severe and shy, a
concrete engineer, he strikes me as one of those communists that the members of the politburo have long
since lost. He speaks slowly, softly, methodically about
the new breed of people who can be encountered in
Siberia. He lives like a modern nomad, going from
one power station to the next with his wife. She is the
daughter of a famous design engineer from Moscow
who belongs to the nomenklatura. He was offered
a big apartment, a career and the privileges that go
with it in the capital; he refused the offer because he
wanted to stay in Siberia.

He talks about a friend who went to North Vietnam to give the people there 'fraternal help' in the war. When the station he built was completed, the Americans bombed it. His colleague survived it but one of his legs was crushed. It was days before he was found in the jungle and flown back home via Hanoi.

A smile on the engineer's face makes his keenness bearable, even attractive. 'Building is difficult,' he says, 'and destroying easy.' The idea that progress comes at a price, has its drawbacks, its horrors, seems far from his mind. Despite that he listens carefully when I explain what I mean by that and promises to think it over.

That night in the hotel I get into conversation with an East German who works in broadcasting, because I complained about the noise from his short-wave radio. He recognizes me. A skinny, flaxen-haired guy whose voice immediately takes on the Saxon tone characteristic of a GDR official unsure of himself: 'Just between ourselves'—'Not that I'm trying to convert you'—'I'm not saying that in my function as such-and-such.' Even when he says something sensible, it sounds insincere. Instead of giving free rein to my prejudices, I offer him the cigar the engineer gave me. He's amazed and hesitates to accept it. How apprehensive he is! I'm even starting to feel sorry for him. God knows how many mouths he has to feed.

I remember the worker in the power house, brooding in his hidey-hole because he has a broken heart, and the sleepy girl at the monitors in the control centre. I suspect that the heroic days are a thing of the past in Bratsk. The 'Heroes of Labour' are already tackling their next project. But soon, it'll just be the bureaucrats who call the shots here.

11 September. Back to Irkutsk by car, across the taiga. A magnificent primeval forest, light, slim, transparent. A wealth of subarctic vegetation: lichens, mushrooms, thistles and little flowers that seem remarkably delicate. Birches, pines, cedars. The most beautiful are the larches with their storm-tousled heads. Fallen trees with charred bark show that the mixed forest is self-regulated with lightning strikes.

After two hours we turn off and continue on foot to the bank of the Angara and find a stinking, foam-covered river that a cellulose combine has turned into liquid manure. 'Man, the pig' (Gottfried Benn)—a remark that is unfair to our domesticated animals. The vegetation and the elemental forces of nature will bury everything our species has built here. It's just matter of time, but that's not much consolation.

The next morning the two-hour journey from Irkutsk to Lake Baikal. It's said to be the deepest lake in the world. More than 1,600 metres, that's accepted as a world record. I can't remember how big it is, nor the huge amount of fresh water it stores.

We're heading for the village of Listvyanka on the shore, close to the place where the Angara from the lake joins the Yenisei that flows into the Arctic Ocean far away to the north. Lake Baikal is one of the wonders of the world. Its water is clear and transparent but much too cold for a swim. It's windy here and colder than farther downstream. It's still bearable now but in winter for months it's freezing at minus 20 degrees.

We are expected at the Limnological Institute of the Academy of Sciences that developed out of a research station established in 1928. Highly competent specialists from all possible disciplines work here: hydrographers, geologists, climatologists, botanists, zoologists, geophysicists . . . Their main function is to observe changes in the environment. They complain about being tied to political apron strings and the lack of technical equipment, but they still have a confusing arsenal of instruments at their disposal. I've no idea what the difference between an actino- and an albedometer is, nor what bathymetry or a pluviograph is. They even have a machine to measure hoar frost.

An old-style wooden building is used as a museum of natural history. The flora and fauna of the region are unique: muskrats and species of seal that only exist here, and fish that are so fat, they melt in the heat of the sun and die if they come too close to the surface. The variety of things I could see here— if we only had more time—makes my head spin.

On the opposite bank snow-covered mountains. On their southern flank the Trans-Siberian Railway continues in an easterly direction to the Pacific. There is smoke rising above Baykalsk. It comes from the huge cellulose and paper factories that, in the long term, will devastate the ecology of the lake. An ecologist at the Institute says, 'When she's grown up my five-year-old daughter won't recognize Lake Baikal.' He's in despair because no one in Moscow will listen to the researchers' alarming results.

The next day back in Irkutsk I met a man who's worth a few paragraphs. He was called Slavo. I can only remember his first name. No wonder, given the pace of this crazy trip anything that's not written down at once is forgotten two days later. Slavo's a writer—not one of the usual kind, however, but an absolute loner who lives with his wife, a teacher, in a sparsely furnished single room. He's a reserved, rather taciturn guy: a straight head, muscular physique and sharp hunter's eyes. In order to survive he has to write for the newspapers they have here and that he hates. He has no money and he probably drinks too much.

In the summer he borrows some money to bribe an air-force pilot to fly him, with sleeping bag, rifle and vodka in his rucksack, a few hundred kilometres north to the Samoyeds who live on their reindeer. The state is far away. The women can only get married once they've had a child. It's immaterial who the father is.

The hunter comes back to the town with his bag: pelts and furs that he sells on the black market. If I should come back to Siberia, he says, he'll take me to his Samoyed village.

As far as publication opportunities are concerned, he tells me, things don't look too good for him. A completed manuscript he shows me is entitled 'Go Far Away and Come Back', and the sequel that he's now working on, 'Stay with Yourself'. He can speak English, is familiar with Hamsun, Faulkner, Salinger and Böll. He tells me how he managed to obtain the only Russian publication of James Joyce: a 1935 volume of *Inostrannaya Literatura*. He has very definite opinions when he talks about literature. 'You have to write as well as the classics.' He is contemptuous of Yevtushenko, especially of the poem he wrote about the Bratsk power station. I too am slowly losing patience with that poet. I wish him no harm, but I can't get rid of the feeling that his prospects are not good: a 'remarkable rocket' that, as it says in

Oscar Wilde's story, shoots up with great effect but will soon fizzle out.

We embrace as we say goodbye. We'll probably never hear from each other again.

13 September. Arrival in Novosibirsk. A hard town which, at first sight, appears to lack urbanity. Marina asks a tall young man the way to the main station. Coarse, reddened features, brown eyes, firm chin. He's hobbling because he fell off his motorbike two months ago. Grigori, as he's called, seems at the same time both boorish and boyish. He shows us the white-painted station proudly, as if he'd built it himself. He just thinks the food in the restaurant is poor; he's not impressed by the Stalinist decor.

There are cupolas, galleries, side rooms, corridors and tunnels. A teeming crowd of peasant women, war veterans in rags, Kirghiz traders, armed police, officers beribboned with decorations, flower sellers and cobblers with bag and baggage full of leather off-cuts, rubber heels and tools. It's busy day and night. Bedding in the subways surrounded by bundles and baskets. A guitarist has set up there. Fewer things are forbidden here than in German stations. The clocks show Moscow time.

An airport will never reach this degree of intimacy of the crowd. The teeming mass of people reminds me of street scenes by Poe and Baudelaire. The aeroplane cannot compete with the magic of the big green trains that, with their samovars and their plush beds beneath the Soviet star, go as far as the Amur River.

As in every large Russian town there is an information office that is supposed to make up for the lack of address and telephone books. But you don't just have to have the first name and surname of the person you're asking about, you also have to have their patronymic and year and place of birth, otherwise, as Marina says, using Kafka's words, you're 'not accepted'.

Grigori, our guide, was born in Novosibirsk and has never left the town. As he tells us over lunch, he lives together with his parents, five brothers and girlfriend 'in the best area, the Kirov district'. They built their wooden house themselves, working in the evening and at weekends, perfectly legally, he claims, with materials they bought. He'd never have set out on such an adventurous project on his own, for he used to be a finisher in mechanical engineering. If he'd stayed with that, he tells us, he would have been able to have a cheap works apartment, but he'd preferred to take a correspondence course in interior decoration. Since then he'd earned his living with cinema posters and window displays; sometimes he made a lot, sometimes very little. He spent his money immediately, he admits, where it went he couldn't say. At such times half the town became his friends. His girlfriend was a steersman (!) on a steamer on the Ob. When it's not running in the winter, she's on half pay but has to commit herself to going back for the next season. He says she's not as irresponsible as he is. He ought not to drink or smoke. She's expecting a child. Most of all he'd like a son. That was his heartfelt wish. He said nothing about a car, a holiday, a TV. He didn't ask me one single question about our standard of living. What moved him to go around the town with us for two hours? He accompanied us to the hotel, where he took his leave with a thin smile.

In the afternoon the town makes an almost southern impression. There are many young people out, as if on a *corso*. Only towards evening does it become cool. In a queue for the cinema, Marina and I get talking to two young women, not much older than 25. They'd never spoken to a foreigner before. Immediately, they want to know where I come from. When I say Germany, one of them asks, '*Nashi?*' By that they mean the GDR where, in Soviet usage, '*our* Germans' live. A visitor from the West is clearly more interesting.

No trace of hostility towards world beyond the Iron Curtain but pride in their own town.

Mara, the older one, works in an aeroplane factory, the other in an electronics institute. Both want to become engineers. Work goes from seven in the morning to four in the afternoon, then night school until ten. In this town of a million inhabitants there's everything that a real metropolis should have— opera house, concert hall, conservatoire and several universities—but no bar, not even an ordinary pub. The only thing we can invite our new friends to is to have an ice cream, there's an ice-cream parlour on every corner in Siberia.

Ala is the name of the younger and more intelligent one. When, asked about my profession, I have to confess to being a poet, that sets off a conversation about poetry. I've long since realized that in Russia this activity enjoys the kind of prestige we can only dream about, but Ala has no intention of idealizing it. When I ask her what she expects of a poet, she replies: honesty.

There's nothing coquettish about it, but the two of them are absolutely determined to continue the conversation. However, it's gradually getting cold in the windy streets, what should we do? Marina pushes us past the porter into the foyer of our hotel. At least it's warm in there.

Now our discussion really gets going. Ala turns out to have a passion for reading. She knows poems by Pushkin, Yesenin, Mandelstam by heart. And what about those of the present day? Marina asks. I mention Yevtushenko. 'Oh him,' is Ala's response. 'He should just go on writing for the newspapers and appearing on television, but I don't believe a word he says.'—'And Andrei Voznesensky?'—'He's certainly better but still not sincere. There's a younger one comes closest, I read something by her in a magazine. It was very good. She's called Bella Akhmadulina. Have you heard of her?'

And so it went on for quite a while. My Russian wasn't good enough to follow the arguments of these critics and Marina was getting weary of translating them. In the long term the energy of these young women will be worth more than all the raw materials of Siberia.

When the porter on duty closed the foyer, Ala suggested we should accompany them back to her lodgings. We walked for a quarter of an hour until we came to an old, dilapidated tenement. Ala whisked us past a grey-haired woman snoring in a glass cubicle. That was the concierge. On the fourth floor Ala opened the door to the apartment without making a sound and tiptoed down a dark corridor smelling of cabbage and disinfectant. There were things piled up along the walls. In the darkness it was impossible to make out whether they were suitcases, household goods or other belongings. The corridor must also have served as a drying room, for we brushed past damp articles of clothing that were hung up. Only at the end of the corridor do we reach Ala's little room. She switched on the light. For the first time I became acquainted with a *kommunalka*.

It is typical that I had never come across this kind of housing on my travels, even though since 1918 it has been the norm for millions of people in the Soviet Union. I had been a guest in cabins and dachas, but also in the kitchens of the intelligentsia where you might meet physicists and composers, people from the theatre and language specialists. In such places there was a characteristic atmosphere of trust and informality. There was much that was understood and didn't need to be expressed explicitly. Ideological clichés were scorned, money was of no great importance, many things that weren't in any newspaper quickly got around.

Things were quite different in a kommunalka. How they were Marina explained to me over breakfast next morning. These communal apartments take in a whole storey, that in the old days a single middle-class family would have occupied. Today a couple of dozen people will live in them, not as a temporary expedient but for years. Often a couple have to share a single room with their children; if necessary a curtain is used to divide the room. The rooms are allocated by the authorities, with no consideration given to how old they are, where they come from, what they have studied or how they earn their living. There's only one lavatory where the tenants have to queue, and one bathroom that's always occupied. Where can you keep your suitcases, your winter boots, your sack of flour, your jars of pickled gherkins? There's no room left in the corridor. It stinks of dishwater and vinegar. There are always quarrels in the kitchen. My fur hat's disappeared, and who stole little Alyona's rag-doll rabbit?

In such an environment it's inevitable that there are bitter arguments over the most everyday tasks, malicious gossip and informing the KGB. No one has counted how many people live in such conditions from which, as Marina tells me, there's only one way out: the high-rise apartments.

Ala's room was crammed full of furniture. We sat down on the bed, on an olive-green wooden bunk and on the floor that was carpeted with cushions. She told us she had to share the little room with her mother, who had gone out to a village to visit a sister who was ill. The stucco roses on the high ceiling indicated that the once much more spacious room had been divided by a thin wall to accommodate new tenants who'd been assigned to the kommunalka.

Dawn was already breaking when we said good-bye to Ala and Mara. While we were still in the doorway the younger of the two asked me if I could live there. That's a question I've been asking myself often enough on this journey. The answer is: Rather not!

When I think about that night, I come to the conclusion that life as experienced by the Soviet citizens puts any Marxist analysis of class relationships in the shade. People in this country are familiar with the subtlest nuances of status, rank and standard of living, and that not merely with regard to the question of accommodation. Who can have his own telephone? Where, it at all, does he go on holiday? Which documents does he have and which ones does he lack? Where does he go when he's ill? In which stores does he do his shopping? Where is he allowed to travel and where not? How does he dress? Where is he studying and what? What kind of shoes does he wear? What does he eat? Does he have a dacha? And what do the women have to put up with? They join a queue when the word goes around: 'They've been throwing shoes,' or soap, or bathing costumes in the winter. The pronoun 'they' stands for some planning authority or other. Mostly the shelves are empty, the window displays pyramids of old tins. You have to queue three times: first for a chit at the counter, then to pay at the cash desk, and finally, to collect your goods. One thing that has been missing from this country for decades is tampon; the planned economy seems to be unaware that there are women living on this earth. No one has been able to explain that to me.

A foreign visitor may ask himself questions such as these and many others but he won't find any answers. And the role played by money in Russia is equally puzzling. When the people I knew talked about it, if at all, it was only in passing. They had nothing but contempt for the high regard in which it is held in Western Europe.

Others, such as Slavo, the Siberian fur hunter, or Ala, who supplied us with tea out of a thermos, had a different attitude. They had to save. But for what? The prices in GUM, at the stations, in the village shops varied inexplicably. Some fat tomes were absurdly cheap. In the large towns, there were shops on every second street corner selling quite decent Crimean champagne at the same price as lemonade. Once I saw a microscope that cost less than a pair of slippers. The price tag would have put any professor of economics in a state of shock. There was no place for Adam Smith in this economic system. My suspicion was that there were other currencies in the Soviet Union apart from the rouble, that self-sufficiency and barter played an important role, that connections and both visible and invisible privileges mattered for everything one needed.

In the hotel, after a late breakfast, a certain Ilya F.
approached us, presumably because he suspected we
were colleagues. In a way he was the counterpart to
the two factory girls the previous evening. He considered himself a poet and therefore, on the model of
painters in films about artists, had a long beard and
wore a beret. An obliging but rather dull person
who'd managed to get his little volumes published in
editions of 3,000 copies each. He's travelled to Mexico
and Vietnam, and to the oil prospectors on the delta
of the Ob and has written commissioned poems and
articles about them. Apart from such standard fare,
he seemed to have nothing to say for himself. Marina
said, 'We too have our own kind of bores who flourish here.'

Not only the members of the intelligentsia, everyone in the Soviet Union uses the first person plural
possessive pronoun in a particular way. They talk of
'our poet', 'our composer', 'our inventor', 'our astro-
naut', etc., even when it's a posthumous appropria-
tion of celebrities whom society gave a hard time
when they were still alive.

14 September. A detour to Akademgorodok. That's
a new town that was founded in the 1950s. It lies on
an immense reservoir to the south of Novosibirsk,
150 kilometres of the Ob have been transformed into
a lake. The town contains 60,000 scientists and is a

kind of brain-combine with a computer centre, smart hotel and bungalows housing the researchers. The landlord is the Academy of Sciences. It has a campus atmosphere with a very good canteen and comfortable libraries. There are steps to a long path which goes through the birchwoods, that recall the classic pictures of Ilya Repin, and to the bathing beach where the scientists relax.

However, the expense of money and materials here does not reach American proportions. The stories about how the members of the Academy are cosseted are exaggerated. However, things are permitted here that are not tolerated elsewhere. On the walls there are lithographs of works by Matisse, Miró and the Surrealists; Socialist Realism has no chance here.

Mostly the scientists speak in English with a strong accent and have travelled to the West, Palo Alto, Princeton, Geneva . . . particle and plasma physicists, mathematicians, geneticists, geologists. They all talk very openly. The boss is a polite apparatchik of modest achievements, probably reporting to the KGB, who is regarded with quiet irony. There is a simple reason why the exercise of authority is different here: the Party depends on these brains to keep up in the armament and technology race. The scientists complain that their computers are out-of-date, not up to the standard of the competition in the West: too slow, not enough storage capacity. The cyberneti-

cists in the computer centre are relaxed, totally unin-
terested in ideology. Politics is discussed at home, if
at all, in the evening and 'for fun' rather than seriously.
No one wants to be a 'Hero of Labour'.

Over a cup of tea, a young geologist explains his
theory of the development of petroleum to me. He
is looking at micromechanical processes on the shore-
lines of vanished oceans. He claims that in geological
time the friction of the tides on the littorals led to the
formation of aromatic carbohydrates. If his hypothesis is correct, it will be of significance in the hectic
search for new deposits that is going on in Siberia at
present.

The most impressive department for me is the
Institute for Cytology and Genetics. Its director is
Raissa Berg, a beautiful woman of perhaps 50 who
doesn't mince her words. She probably has a Jewish
background.

Her most important teacher was none other than
Hermann Muller, an American communist and later
Nobel laureate who worked in the Soviet Union for
four years and was very keen on eugenics. Under him
she studied population genetics and continued his
experiments in mutation. Drosophila was the preferred object of these experiments. Then Lysenko got
in her way. He was Stalin's favourite, a narrow-minded
agronomist who denounced genetics as a 'bourgeois
science'. That had disastrous consequences. In 1946

there was an ideologically motivated campaign that drove Raissa Berg out of her Moscow Institute. Not until the 'thaw' was it possible for her to continue her experiments. Recently she was appointed to Akadem-gorodok. I believe she is determined to see to it that the free pursuit of science is possible in Russia again. No one who has encountered her can doubt her combative temperament. Clearly a kind of intellectual opposition has formed in her circle.

While she's talking, I remember my old plans to write essays and reports on the history of the sciences. That gives a layman like myself privileged access to the contradictions of research—examples: Brecht's play *The Life of Galileo*, Thomas Kuhn's investigations into the 'development of the new'. I would love to go back to those topics I used to deal with on the radio.

On the last evening we're entertained by the mathematician Alexander Danilovich Alexandrov, not in the Institute but in his private residence. It turns into a long conversation. He's Einstein-like with a certain German slant, a shock of white hair and a powerful nose. A mix of earnestness, fantasy, charm and self-irony. For 12 years he was rector of Leningrad University. A Stalin Prize protected him against the repression. Works on quantum mechanics, differential geometry and crystal structure. He has, he says, been working on a problem of convex surfaces for 29 years but only found partial solutions. Then he talks about the Hausdorff Theorem, about which I understand nothing. He describes how you can split a sphere into four parts and create two new spheres from them.

Mathematics as the 'queen of sciences'? Alexandrov is sceptical about that. He considers the assertion that it is of enormous benefit to society a standard fabrication. 'It has no truths to give us.' At least it does require proofs, a demand, he says, that is invaluable in times when the politicians arrogate more and more power to themselves.

He loves discussing so much that he forgets about time. I get worked up about the fact that the high-school curriculum contains none of the things that have happened in mathematics since infinitesimal calculus: no combinatorics, no topology, no group theory . . . His reply is that it's entirely understandable. Since most people's capacity for abstract thought is insufficient to keep up with them, such a cultural delay is normal and inevitable.

But is it not extremely dangerous to take political action without knowing what we are doing, that is, without insight into the consequences? 'Our consciousness is moulded prior to the encounter with science,' he says, 'and that's not going to change.' Fermi, he goes on, was in favour of dropping the atom bomb on Japan, although what that meant was clearer to him than to others. I mention the pilots of the strategic force Bomber Command. We agree on the conclusion that knowledge and moral imagination are at best complementary.

In the evening we drive back across the smoky steppes under a low sky. The sprawling city beyond tall chimneys with black smoke belching out.

During the night I undertake one more voyage of discovery, going on my own by tram through broad streets and dark districts. The same names everywhere in Russia: Marx Prospect, Komsomol Square, Proletarskaya, Lenin Street. Extensive *terrain vague* between residential quarters and factories. Out of curiosity I risked boarding one of the Ob steamers that was moored at the landing stage. I only got back on land at the last minute when the hooter sounded before the boat cast off. Otherwise I'd have spent 24 hours going down the river with no possibility of getting back.

17/18 September. From Novosibirsk to Moscow on the Trans-Siberian Railway. 'To Moscow!' At last! The journey is more monotonous than the myth that promises adventures of all kinds on this route. After weeks on the move, the time differences in this country are starting to take it out of me. After all, it is five hours between Irkutsk and Moscow. After the hectic way I've been flying around this country, jetlag has started making me feel depressed.

At least I have a compartment in the 'soft class', with a little lamp swathed in pleated pink material. In the corridor I meet men smoking and wearing striped pyjamas that they keep on during the day. There is a Japanese couple going to Moscow who try to document the emptiness outside the window with their camera. Now and then the train stops, God knows why, at a deserted station consisting of a barely illuminated shack and a water crane. No town or village is to be seen, just a statue of Lenin with his right hand stretched out as if he were hitching a lift. At any time of day or night you can get a cup of hot tea from a babushka at the end of the coach; it's in a glass that sits in a silver-plated beaker. You're given a sugar cube with it. If you follow the local custom, you stick it in your mouth and slurp up the tea to sweeten it. There's also a restaurant car in which two demure ladies are knitting, while workers in padded jackets are tucking into borscht at the next table. Finally we cross the bridge over the Volga at Yaroslavl. The passengers start to stow their food and luggage away in bundles and suitcases. They know it's not far to Moscow now, a mere 300 kilometres—a stone's throw.

18 September. In the capital I don't miss the well-meant supervision I've been lumbered with so far any more than an official programme. I still had a 'good visa' in my passport and the spacious room in the Peking was at my disposal, but I had no intention of using it. Instead I set off for a quite different address: 19 Lavrushinsky pereulok, on the south side of the Moscow canal, quite close to the Tretyakov Gallery. With a Metro map I'd managed to get hold of it was easy—three stops to Novokuznetskaya Station. It was something special for me to explore this means of transport that is as magnificent as it's cheap. A few kopeks and you're in, gliding down long escalators to the depths, where you find yourself in vaults decorated with frescoes, reliefs and statues, in a style in which tsarist splendour and communist iconography have formed a strange alliance.

Only in the long, draughty, dirty passageways does it look different. They are the location for a not-quite-legal but tolerated and thriving trade in flowers, newspapers, handmade articles and, probably, smuggled goods. Why is it here of all places that I recall something I had read in a book by Hannah Arendt? 'The claim that only Moscow has an underground railway is only a lie as long as the Bolsheviks don't have the power to destroy all other underground railways. Only in a completely controlled and ruled world can a totalitarian dictator ignore all facts, turn all lies into reality and make all prophecies come true.'

Such insights were not what I had in mind. I rang the bell at one of the lavish buildings that had been specially constructed for members of the nomen-klatura in the 1930s. I'd told Masha that I was coming. I was expected in Margarita Aliger's family home. It was spacious and comfortable, but far from the cos-mopolitan ambience Ehrenburg had displayed. Old furniture, old memories, an old clock, a Finnish chest of drawers, an old tartan travelling rug. It didn't look like privileged ostentation here, but hard work and modesty, as if in a time capsule that contained many things I didn't know about.

But, above all, Masha was there; now we set about making plans, and not just for the next seven days. For however friendly her mother's welcome, she knew her daughter. With the result that she wasn't just concerned, she was worried. What was going to come of this liaison with a visitor from the West? Did Masha, perhaps, want to go abroad with him?

It was Marina Pavchinskaya who came to our aid. Along with Kostya and Lev, she turned out to be another who brought good fortune. She knew Margarita, she knew how to deal with awkward situ-ations and out of her pocket she took the key to an apartment where we could be together undisturbed.

Masha's mother had no objection to an excursion to Peredelkino, so that's how I got to know that legendary place. You take the Elektrichka for a good quarter of an hour to the south-west. The station resembles a wooden shed. Here too, equality has remained an empty promise; substantial villas stand beside crooked shacks. The only things that aren't missing, even on the poorer huts, are the TV aerials. On arriving you might, if you're lucky, find a carriage to take you along an avenue of pines and past villas to Margarita's dacha on the edge of the woods.

The place is like something out of a short story by Chekhov. There I got to know the real ruler of the holiday house. The faithful Nyanya had been Masha's wet-nurse, then her nanny and now, over 70, she lights the stove, sees to the upkeep if the house, looks after the goats, feeds the dogs, gives Lyova, the ancient tomcat, its milk and puts the samovar on for the visitors.

This old woman has always been there, through the starvation years and the purges, through Stalinism and the Second World War. She's seen Margarita's failed marriages and love affairs, and been through the deaths, moments of happiness and suicides in the family. She's also looked after Masha when her mother was away during the siege of Leningrad or with the army or, later, when she was writing at her desk or on her travels to Chile, to Paris or to Alma-Ata.

At the dacha was a big old Saint Bernard called Egri. How Nyanya managed to get him through the difficult times and feed him, I have no idea. In the Soviet Union, where meat is hard to find and expensive, something like that counts as a luxury that only a few can afford. I've never been particularly fond of dogs, but this Egri had a dignity that I liked. He didn't bark at me, he didn't stink, he didn't lick you up and down; he was a gentleman of his species. We went on walks with him in the woods, looked for mushrooms and berries, and enjoyed the peace and quiet together.

It was only later that I wanted to know more precisely what made this Peredelkino the place it was. In the 1930s, Maxim Gorky saw to it that the whole of this rural area was transferred to the Litfond, the property administration of the all-powerful Writers' Association that had a colony of over 50 summer-holiday-houses built for its authors. Thus many well-known writers found a home from home in a few square kilometres at the gates of Moscow. They formed a strange commune, such as is only conceivable in Russia. Was it quieter here or more dangerous? Was it easier for them to write here or were they easier to keep under surveillance where the Simonovs, Fedins and Tchaikovskys lived almost cheek by jowl with the deviationists. Right next door to the house where Masha's father, the awful Fadeyev, shot himself, Pasternak lived and worked, until his death six years ago, in a villa to which his admirers make pilgrimage, as they do to his grave. They stand by the fence, as if they were at a shrine, in silence, then they go on. 'Peredelkino', a cycle of poems from 1941, shows Pasternak's attachment to this place.

It's impossible as you pass by to note even the names of all those who are remembered here: suspicious characters and those who escaped, the famous and the forgotten . . . Did Ilf and Petrov live here? Isaac Babel, Yuri Olesha, Boris Pilnyak, Veniamin Kaverin, Andrei Platonov? I don't know. The only ones I'm sure about are Konstantin Paustovsky and Lydia Chukovskaya, who were close friends of Masha's mother, for I had the good fortune to meet them.

Then it's back by the suburban train to Margarita's apartment. Communication with her has never been a problem for me, and not only because she speaks French, English and even a little German. It's not simply due to her charm, either, but to her attitude that she has maintained through all the catastrophes in her country. She has even managed to preserve a touch of naivety. Sometimes I see her as a biblical figure and then the little girl inside her reappears. In the long run she was incapable of clinging on to the delusions of her colleagues and fellow citizens. The

massacre of her political illusions was a gradual process. It's difficult to say where all the wounds end up
as resignation and where wisdom begins. Courage
she has never lacked. There are no hymns to Stalin
from her pen. In the years of the 'Thaw' she managed
to get poems by Akhmatova, Pasternak and Marina
Tsvetaeva published.

She doesn't respond to repression with loud
protests but, with a gesture out of the Torah, raises
her eyes to the heavens and quietly shrugs her shoulders. When the first dissidents were arrested in Red
Square, she felt that justice was on their side but their
demonstrations struck her as too theatrical. Cynicism
is entirely foreign to her. From the very first day I have
admired and revered Margarita Aliger.

God knows whether anyone is keeping a watch on
our comings and goings; whether they turn a blind
eye in the office of the Writers' Association when my
room in the Peking is unoccupied. Masha's mother is
worried about the way we're going on. Even my faithful guide Marina warns us, 'You're not registered anywhere.' Where should we be? I ask in return. Once
again I'm the clueless one, the ignoramus. What are
we in for now?

On top of all that was the *Itinerary* in my official
travel schedule that was unrelenting: a short trip to

Georgia. That was all I needed. I'd had enough of after-dinner speeches and discussions about world peace, about Socialist or any other Realism. No more sightseeing, no more toasts and no more airports!

Why shouldn't I simply throw the association's well-meant intentions back in their face? Play the arrogant Westerner and cancel everything? Was the beginning of my Russian novel nothing more than just an escapade? Masha, who was always more determined than I was, said nothing but my hesitation brought silent reproaches from her. And she turned a deaf ear to the objections of her mother and her friends. Nor did the fact that we were both married bother her in the least. She was determined to get a divorce from her husband, who was already over the hills and far away. 'That's nothing more than a piece of paper,' she said. Much more important to her, she went on, was to have a proper passport in her pocket as soon as possible. That's what she was going to see to during the few days that, like it or not, I had to spend in Georgia.

On **25 September** I arrived in Tiflis, that is now called Tbilisi. My stay there is full of gaps—I was too tired to make more than a few brief notes. I was transported to Georgia, for which there is also a Soviet name: Gruzinskaya, even though my ability to take things in had long since been exhausted. I certainly didn't travel alone but I can't remember who accompanied me. Was it Marina or was it Kostya?

The official reason was an anniversary. Shota Rustaveli is the Georgian national poet. I think it was 800 years that had passed since his birth or death. No idea which. I've never read one line of his epic poem. It's called *The Knight in the Panther's Skin* and is said to be pretty long. In my suitcase I find a commemorative medal weighing a kilogram that had been given to me and that I will secretly forget somewhere.

I was so fed up with official state ceremonies that whenever possible I slipped away and used the time to go for walks around the old town, take a nap on a park bench or stock up on grapes, plums and apricots in the market. Anyone coming from Moscow is amazed at the abundance here. The Georgians are not only corrupt, they're rich. A strange empire where the capital turns out to be more impoverished than the provinces!

The next day I was dragged off to Gori by my hosts. A journey of more than two hours to the west. It had to be because this one-horse town is the birthplace of Iosif Vissariononovič Džugašvili (I had to get the correct transliteration of his name from the encyclopedia). Stalin, as you can see, is still revered in Georgia. Anyone who has a car sticks a portrait of him on the windscreen. He stands about 20 metres high outside the town hall of this small place that probably makes its living from tourism. Visitors are carted off to a monstrous museum. What is claimed to be the house where he was born looks fake. A huge building houses the pipes, the uniforms and the death mask of the dictator. Best of all, however, is an extensive collection of presents from all over the world, given to him by grateful comrades. There's not just the usual kitsch produced for government gifts. More interesting are little self-made model mines, rockets, flower mosaics, embroidered coloured portraits . . . all with little labels recording the names of the donors together with place and date.

And that wasn't all. I was taken on to a spa famous for its mineral springs. It's called Borjomi. Old villas and mansions from the time of the tsars. The mineral water is a warm, salty, stinking liquid to which miraculous powers are ascribed. Tolstoy is said to have drunk it.

All I can remember of the dinner in the capital, Tbilisi, is that my scholarly hosts' knowledge of German was impressive and the Georgian dishes exquisite. Later that evening, I tumbled into my bed, benumbed by the celebrated Georgian brandy that can stand comparison with cognac.

On **30 September** I was finally back in Moscow. Farewell to Masha, to Margarita, to Kostya and Marina with no idea when I'd see them again.

Two days later I flew back to Oslo and returned to my family. In my luggage I had a 70-by-30-centimetre tome weighing over 4 kilograms that I had exchanged for my last rouble notes: the splendid *Physical-Geographic Atlas of the World*, published by the Academy of Sciences and the Central Office for Geodesy and Cartography of the Soviet Union, Moscow, 1964. Resplendent on the black cloth binding is a globe adorned with the hammer and sickle, crowned with a star, wreathed with ears of corn and wrapped in a banner on which it says in 15 languages: 'Workers of the world unite.' Its 249 plates present a view of the world that is as colourful and as detailed as any lover of the planet could wish for: tectonics, air and water temperatures, vegetation, fauna, demography, insolation, precipitation, glaciology, mineral resources . . . No question is left unanswered in this magnificent volume, which cannot be matched either in the USA or in Europe. And all that for a derisory 40 roubles!

For many years I'd been living with my Norwegian wife Dagrun and our daughter Tanaquil on Tjøme, an island between Tønsberg Fjord and Oslo Fjord. We'd bought a little white sea-captain's house with a large garden. Below is a poem evoking the tenor of our life there:

Calm were the northern evenings in June, /

carefree the chime of the brass clock on the
island, / forgetful stood the wooden house,
a haven of peace, / in which it never grew
dark, / calm, calm lay the boat at the jetty, /
as if happiness had been there, calm / stood
the books, the rocks, bright on the shelf /
stood the brandy.

But for some time now, I'd had the feeling that
something was about to happen in Germany. There
were signs that things were about to fall apart in the
Federal Republic. The long-established authoritarian
state with its leftovers from the days of the kaiser and
its persistent heritage from the dictatorship was no
longer viable. In the hope that sooner or later it would
become a country that was fit to live in again, I had,
with the help of Uwe Johnson who lived in the neighbourhood, bought a house in Friedenau. Our plan
was to spend the summer in Norway and the winter
in Berlin.

But now a flood of love-letters and telegrams
arrived from Moscow. I could no longer keep quiet
about my Russian novel. A separation was unavoidable. I felt like a burglar who unthinkingly smashes
everything to bits. Without destructive energy it's
impossible to disregard your own rules.

In addition to all that I had established a periodical
that couldn't really be directed from a distance. That
would have been unthinkable without the learned

editor, Karl Markus Michel, who was intelligent enough never to deign to take an academic examination. He remained faithful to *Kursbuch* throughout the trials and tribulations it was to encounter.

The Grand Coalition had brought the political situation in Germany to the point where the Republic had no effective opposition. Together, the CDU and the SPD had concocted the so-called Emergency Laws, an outrageous piece of business that we refused to go along with. We, an extra-parliamentary minority, that didn't consist simply of a few thousand students, old communists loyal to Moscow plus some hippies. There were still some liberals left but, above all, a powerful wing of the trade unions that took a stand against these laws. In October 1966, they called for a demonstration on Römer Square in Frankfurt with the slogan 'Emergency for Democracy'. I believe the speakers there were Ernst Bloch, Helmut Ridder and Georg Benz of the Metalworkers' Union. All of them honourable men!

I was so furious that I allowed myself to be talked into giving a speech to 25,000 people. It was terrible for, in the middle of my tirade, I realized I was capable whipping up the crowd, that was already aroused, even more. I was so disgusted with myself that I called the country a banana republic, saying, 'All those sitting in their parliamentary bunker over there are really trembling!' And I don't take back a single word of it.

But the loudspeakers sent back a booming echo from all sides and I suddenly remembered: where had I encountered this overheated atmosphere before? Had not the voice of that rabble-rouser in the Berlin Sportpalast, 25 years ago, sounded similar? I was well on the way to becoming a demagogue. It was a nauseating feeling, no matter whether my arguments were right or wrong. I finished the speech as best I could and swore never to speak on a platform again. It's a promise I have kept. I'd been inoculated against large-scale demonstrations.

10 December 1966 was a Saturday. A few Berlin students, including my brother Ulrich, put on a farcical show on the Kurfurstendamm in Berlin that turned out to have serious consequences. They protested against the Vietnam War by throwing confetti and singing Christmas carols. 'We're demonstrating for the police,' they announced. 'We demand modern equipment for them: instead of rubber truncheons a white tin with sweets for children who are crying and condoms for teenagers who want to make love.' The police could think of nothing better than to indulge in an orgy of beating. Exactly one week later, the little group repeated their peaceful guerrilla tactics while mingling with people taking a walk.

This time demonstrators, tourists, women pensioners were battered indiscriminately by policemen for whom it was just too much and who'd lost all control. More than 80 people who were simply out for a walk, including children and housewives, were arrested.

Their provocative action brought the organizers not just an arrest but their first big media hit. The street theatre of 1967 had begun. I wasn't there. Again I was somewhere else.

POSTSCRIPT

(2014)

A blue pocket dictionary I took to Russia with me turned out to be pretty useless. As far as possible I had to resort to other languages, mostly English, French and Spanish. Otherwise I was entirely dependent on my friends.

The volume of poems that Lev Ginzburg translated was actually printed but never published. The edition was pulped.

After my return to Berlin I wrote the following poem that can be regarded as a kind of review of my journey:

Peace Congress

A plane lands with a hundred liars on board.
The town bids them welcome with a
      handful of flowers,
with a smell of naphtha and sweat,
with a wind from the steppes of Asia.

In the spotlights' glare the liars say

in fifty languages: We're against war.
Silently I admit the liars are right.
What the liars say is the truth, but
why do we need fifty hours
for a single sentence?

When they leave, the flowers are grey,
the ashtrays overflowing
with fraternal fag ends
unwavering cigar ash
and invincible butts.
Peace is floating around in the spittoons.

In the White House, in the spotlight's glare,
at the same hour the honest people are
        announcing
a different truth: War is on the increase.
Only the liars are unwavering.

In the White House the flowers are fresh,
the spittoons disinfected
and the ashtrays as clean as bombs.

A gust of wind blows across the city,
a wind from the steppes of Asia—like the
        whistle
of a throttled woman, fighting for her life.
The *Kursbuch* of 9 July 1967 published a dossier
on the theme of 'Kronstadt 1921 or the Third Revo-

lution'. I had done the compilation and commentary myself without giving thought to my colleagues in the Moscow Writers' Association. But, busy bees that they were, they passed their discovery on. The consequence was the immediate loss of my status as a 'progressive bourgeois writer'. I can't say exactly how I was categorized from that point on, but clearly I didn't end up in the Inferno of 'anti-Soviet forces'; otherwise, I would presumably never have been granted a visa again.

In 1976, I heard from Moscow that my friend Kostya had died. He was struck down at his door in the stairwell. It is a murder that has never been cleared up. No one seems to know whether it was common criminals, who wanted to ransack his apartment, or a politically motivated crime.

Raissa Berg was one of the signatories of the 1967 'Letter of the Forty-six', that raised objections to the government's violations of human rights. Obstinate as she was, she lost her position in Akademgorodok at the end of the so-called 'Thaw'. In 1974, she decided to emigrate to the USA, where she continued with her research at the universities of Wisconsin and St Louis. In 1988 she published her memoirs, *Acquired Traits: Memoirs of a Geneticist from the Soviet Union*. She was still active politically and supported the dissidents. She died in Paris in 2006.

I'm 85, more or less. How things used to be is a question I'm sometimes asked by my young wife Katharina, my daughters, or a journalist or some student who needs abbreviations such as Dr or MA after his name and has to deliver a thesis for them.

Such information is hard to come by from me. My memory's like a sieve in which very little gets stuck. It's not my age that's the problem—so far I've been spared the famous disease that's made a name for itself, under that of Alois Alzheimer.

However, my interest in writing an autobiography leaves something to be desired. I absolutely have no wish to make a mental note of everything that happens to me. It is with reluctance that I leaf through the memoirs of my contemporaries. I don't trust them one inch. You don't have to be a criminologist or an epistemologist to know that you can't rely on people's testimonies on their own behalf. The transitions between a deliberate lie and tacit improvement, between a simple mistake and subtle self-presentation are difficult to determine. For example, the celebrated *Confessions* of Rousseau, one of the founding fathers of the genre. Other autobiographies sound as if they'd been written by a ghost-writer.

Keep clear of that kind of exercise, I told myself. And I would have stuck to my methodological scruples, had I not, in my cellar one day, happened to come across something that surprised me. Between the wine-rack and my tool-chest a few cardboard boxes were sleeping the sleep of the just. Looking for an old contract, I opened them and found forgotten letters, notebooks, photos, newspaper cuttings, abandoned manuscripts. It was a mass of papers in which any links were purely fortuitous. But at least there was nothing in this jumble that had been invented after a substantial lapse of time.

So I got caught up in jotters and folders from the 1960s and 70s. Could I still do something with this raw material? Such an attempt would not be consistent with my own views, but then consistency was never my strong point. It was worth a try.

The traces I found were sketchy and often hard to decipher. The easiest to deal with was the material from 1963. I found jottings that only needed minimal stylistic revision to remove careless slips. More problematic were the 'scribbled notes' from 1966. In that section there is no question of a scrupulously precise reproduction of those texts. Abbreviated sentences have been completed, undecipherable passages deleted, spelling mistakes corrected. I have left some stupid bits as they are, erased intimate matters. The dates on the notes are those of my itinerary, not of the point when they were written. That was often done after the lapse of a few days, in the hotel or while travelling, whenever I had a quarter of an hour free. Here and there I have augmented this patchwork with additional material from letters, calendars and press reports of 1966.

The 'Memories of a Tumult' sticks even less closely to the standards required for documentation or even for literary research. Between 1967 and 1970 I simply lacked the time, interest and desire to keep a regular diary. Anyway, no one can record everything on a scale of 1:1. That would bring in the well-known cartographic paradox: the map of an area that was as precise as the place it depicts, would simply duplicate reality and thus be superfluous. (That, by the way, is the weakness of all power fantasies that dream of total surveillance.) So, *caveat lector!*

Also, the person I encountered in the papers I found in the cellar was a stranger to me. That 'I' was a different man. I could see only one possible way of approaching him—through a dialogue with a double, who seemed to me like a younger brother I hadn't thought of for a long time. Whether this man, just turned 40, was wrestling with feelings of guilt or awkward situations, whether he was right or wrong, was a matter of indifference to me. That was his affair. He had to deal with it himself. The only thing I was interested in was his answers to the question, 'My dear chap, what did you mean by all that?'

The 'postscripts' simply add details that were unknown to the author at the time of writing. (It's all very well to say things with hindsight. You are perhaps older and wiser, but you tend to think you know better.) Anyone who went through the old times that are dealt with here needn't bother with these supplementary details.

MEMORIES OF A TUMULT

(1967–1970)

Neither of the two of us recognizes himself in the other. Where's this conversation supposed to get us? Is it a trick to winkle out some information? Do you want to interview me?

But you're not a journalist.

Oh, it's simpler than you think.

We'll argue; we'll get tangled up in contradictions.

That doesn't matter. I have just one question for you. Can you explain to me what you were up to back then?

No. I've forgotten most of it and didn't understand the most important bits.

Tell me everything. I'd like you to begin at the beginning and bring this old story to a conclusion.

The memories you're demanding can only come in one form—a collage. And the problem with that is: how can I distinguish the objective tumult from the subjective one? My memory, that delirious, chaotic director, delivers an absurd film with sequences that don't fit together. The sound isn't synchronized with the picture. Whole takes are underexposed. Sometimes all the screen shows is frames of black film. Lots of episodes are shot with a wobbly handheld camera. I don't recognize most of the actors.

That's the way it ought to be.

It's a *Wirrwarr.*

Yes, a Wirrwarr, *a word no other language can match. Two syllables that echo each other for situations where nothing fits together. It sums up a hopeless mess better than the weak* muddle, *the bland* pêle-mêle *and the whimsical* guazzabuglio.

Oh, do stop going on at me with your foreign words!

What I can't quite understand is how so much could happen in a thousand days.

It's as if the director were constantly staggering along. The images jump to and fro through time and place. And yet something must have been going on at the points where the film has been spliced, people were taking action, intriguing, inventions were being made, poems appeared, resolutions, crimes . . . There are people who preserve everything neatly in bottles and make memoirs from it. How they go about it is a mystery to me.

It would be best if we started with your Russian novel. What happened next with you and Masha?

That's private business. Why do you ask such intrusive questions about my love life, that's hardly of interest to anyone, when quite different things were at stake?

Because without your Russian woman no one will understand where you ended up, both physically and politically. Me included.

Do we have to? *Mon coeur mis à nu*—my heart laid bare—that's not of public interest. But OK, if you insist. This is the way it was: I couldn't resist Maria Alexandrovna. And she was prepared to give up everything she was accustomed to for my sake: to break off her marriage, that was on the rocks anyway; to leave her mother's house; and to follow me, a man she'd only known for a few months, to a country she hardly knew anything about and where a foreign language was spoken.

Like all Russians she loved the place where she'd grown up; but every member of her generation, whatever their political outlook, has a Soviet self inside them. And Masha wanted to get rid of that because she could no longer bear the regime she was subject to. The absolute commitment with which she pursued this goal bewitched and terrified me.

She wanted to start a 'new life' with me. Neither of us knew what that meant, but Masha was not deterred by the obstacles she knew would be put in her way. In fact, they spurred her on.

In order to leave the country the first thing she needed was permission from the Soviet authorities. Only the OWIR could grant that.

The OWIR? Never heard of it.

You can't remember how things were back then? That was the notorious 'Visa and Registration Department,' that came under the Ministry of the Interior and that, of course, meant the KGB. It was only from them that Masha could get a passport and an exit visa. Actually, I ought to have known that, for every foreigner was obliged to report to the authorities by the third day of their stay at the latest. Without that stamp in your passport you could encounter all sorts of problems. I had never complied with that regulation, I knew nothing about it. God knows who can have vouched for me. Without realizing it, I was always in a kind of twilight zone when I was going around Moscow.

Naturally our fervent desire was only intensified by all these difficulties. A man of my age will never be prepared to obey a power that wants to forbid him to live with the woman he loves. That always was and ever will be the case.

It soon became clear that there was no possibility of Masha emigrating as long as we weren't married. And for that it was necessary to have the agreement of her mother, who wasn't exactly over the moon about Masha's plans—she didn't want to lose her daughter to a foreigner whom she didn't know that well. But I got on well with Margarita and managed to convince her. She gave in and was prepared to use her connections. She not only knew influential people in the powerful Writers' Association, her contacts went right up to the Central Committee of the ruling party. I didn't understand much about all this background activity. However, the German ambassador in Moscow knew what to do in such delicate cases and promised to help us in his personal capacity if need be.

You're going on as if it were some authority or other, tedious officials, incomprehensible regulations that were responsible for your dilemma. Yet, you were married yourself.

Of course. To Dagrun.

A touch of bigamy, then?

What's this meant to be? A confession?

Not at all, my dear fellow. You're not going to get absolution from me. But no reproaches either. I'm having a look from a safe distance at how you behaved.

It was, above all, because of our daughter Tanaquil that I didn't find it easy to contemplate divorce. Even a pedant like you can understand that.

I began dashing to and fro between Berlin, Norway and Moscow. For months we had to entrust our feelings to the post and the telephone. Almost every day Masha wrote letters to me full of impassioned yearning or sent me telegrams.

Do you still have those letters? Then let her speak for herself.

I wouldn't dream of letting you or anyone else get their grubby fingers on Masha's letters. But one thing did strike me soon enough. She was having considerable difficulty with her studies and couldn't get her dissertation finished. She fell into a kind of panic every time she was faced with an examination. At such times her will power, that had so impressed me, just drained away. Intoxicated by Masha's determination, disturbed by feelings of guilt because of my Norwegian family and distracted by the political upheaval, I didn't take Masha's changes of mood seriously.

And there was another warning sign that I ignored. Once she asked me to bring her a list of medicines that were unobtainable in Moscow. There was nothing unusual about that—everyone who came from abroad or was allowed to travel abroad received such requests. That was why I assumed that the pills she was asking for—they were psychotropic drugs such as Librium and Tryptizol in large quantities—were destined for relatives or friends, perhaps, for her older sister, Tanya, who was talented and beautiful but also irresponsible and emotionally unstable.

That just shows how blind I was. Only later, when I saw those things on her bedside table, did I realize that she was dependent on those pills. In such cases, doctors talk of bipolar disorders and panic attacks because old concepts such as fear, high spirits and sadness seem unscientific. I reproach myself for not having realized how endangered my beloved was. If I'd paid heed to her handwriting, instead of just her words, her condition would have been clear to me. Sometimes her writing was jerky and confused, at other, bold, full of confidence and self-assurance.

Did she cry?

As if you didn't know! It was bad enough. We were both in limbo, she in Moscow, I in West Berlin.

There 1967 began with a small but remarkable innovation. On 1 January, Kommune 1 was founded. The name is said to have come from Rudi Dutschke, who, however, never lived in it. To my ear it sounded pretentious since it referred to the Paris Commune of 1871 and was intended to upstage the Communist Party. Those who set it up liked to pin golden Mao badges, proclaiming the Cultural Revolution in China, to their chests. Then they moved into my house in Friedenau, which happened to be empty at the time.

You were off on your travels again.

Yes. In Rome, in Catania and in Syracuse.

Why, actually?

I can't remember. I came back to find my house occupied by people such as Dieter Kunzelmann, Rainer Langhans and Fritz Teufel. In all seriousness they said, 'Join us. The commune's the solution.' That was the last thing I'd do. It was an absolute nightmare. I chucked the whole lot of them out at once.

So where could Kommune 1 go? It was known in Berlin that for some time Uwe Johnson had been living in New York. One of the members of the Kommune had the idea of moving into his apartment. My little brother Ulrich, who was one of them, even had a proper tenancy agreement with him.

He'd got together with Dagrun, my wife. Some people confuse our voices on the telephone, but that's not right, he was always quite different from me. Younger and less settled. He was kind to her, steadied and comforted her.

However, I found it difficult to see gentle Dagrun as a member of a Berlin commune, but how could I make objections to her decisions? I had no right to do that. She wasn't a person to seek revenge. But as far as our daughter Tanaquil was concerned—she was 10 at the time—I remained inflexible. 'You can visit her and she can visit you as often as you like. But, for the moment she's staying with me. We'll go shopping, we'll do the cooking, we'll tidy up. So you don't need to worry.'

On 2 February we got a divorce by mutual consent without appearing in court ourselves; we were represented by Horst Mahler, who certainly made an impression on the presiding judge with his student-fraternity manner and officer's-mess tone. I was granted custody of Tanaquil.

A regular procedure in the middle of the tumult.

That naturally did not impress the Kommune.

Do we really have to go back to that bunch of morons? I believe there's already a couple of feet of shelf-space full of books about them that are quite rightly designated as secondary literature.

Just a moment! You underestimate the potential of those people.

A few muddle-headed idiots you can count on the fingers of one hand. Everything they had to offer was second- or third-hand. A bit of Proudhon, Wilhelm Reich and Henry Miller, a pinch of Dada and a few quotes from the Situationists'

stock. Definitely more Marx Brothers than Marx. A handful
of failed artists, if you ask me. You're only bringing them
up because you happened to be in the vicinity, because your
Norwegian wife and your brother Ulrich had joined them
and because they ruined your fragile relationship with Uwe
Johnson.

You've never understood what it was all about.

Then you tell me!

Let's begin with the phenomenal success of these
people. In no time at all they managed to get everyone against them. First and foremost middle-class
society, of course, because they mocked property, the
family, the law and religion. But the left-wing was outraged as well. The SDS, that represented left-wing students, expelled them with immediate effect; the GDR
closed its barriers and the countless cadre parties of
the extreme left-wing denounced them as counter-
revolutionaries. With their street-theatre ideas they
got rid of all the theory-mongers in no time at all.
Even the ones who planted bombs felt insulted, for
the three or four members of the Kommune shed
no blood whatsoever, used make-up rather than
Molotov cocktails. They were good at perplexing the
general run of citizens and making their blood boil,
but they didn't want to kill anyone. Future terrorists
dismissed them as amateurs. Instead of taking a shot

at state prosecutors, one day a minor sympathizer literally shat on the court.

Only the media were enthusiastic. For years Kommune 1 provided the press with headlines and increased circulation. And they supplied splendid pictures for TV. On the one hand, the little group received death threats, on the other, the media turned them into pop icons. Their staging was absolutely professional. The exploited all so-called perversions and gratified the public's sadistic and exhibitionist inclinations.

Moreover, the relationship between the Kommune and the popular press was a mutually profitable piece of business. The organizers had a sign on the door of the house: 'First the dough, then the show'. Every interview and every shoot cost money. Thus, the journalists paid their rent and kept their fridge full.

But Langhans, Kunzelmann, Teufel & Co. led the way in another respect. They were the first to do something about abolishing the idea of private life. They probably didn't realize what they'd done by that. A whole industry followed in their footsteps. Private TV channels, that refuse to accept the right to privacy, copied their formula and made a mint out of the formats they developed from it. Since then no voyeur, no exhibitionist needs to go to some old building in Berlin to realize themselves. Pressing a button suffices.

Pretty double-edged, your tribute to the Kommune.

You know that I had quite different problems of my own. In Moscow Masha was busy trying to finish her degree at the Faculty of Language and Literature and was in despair over her dissertation that she just couldn't get finished. The submission date was getting close, she was in a high state of nerves. She finally passed the examination on 21 January.

You waited.

Yes. I was impatient. I'd got into the habit of solving my problems with the help of geography.

What's that supposed to mean?

Nothing makes time pass more quickly than a change of place. One day I was at the airport in New Delhi. I knew next to nothing about India. In the afternoon, there were Victorian invitations to high tea at five on the dot. In Varanasi, I looked on the life-giving waters of the murky Ganges and saw the burning corpses on the ghats. I tried to avoid the other sights people wanted to show me.

The only person I knew in India was a lanky blond sociologist, who had no longer been able to stand things at home. Some NGO had sent him as an aid worker and researcher to Uttar Pradesh; he was to study a village community there. 'Why don't you

look me up when you're in India?' he'd said in Berlin
and given me a telephone number in New Delhi.
When I arrived, there was a note for me at the hotel.
He promised to pick me up the next day.

There was no road, just a dusty cart track. Travelling on his motorbike we went over ruts and pot-
holes, past pack-donkeys and heavily laden women,
for two or three hours until we came to his village.
There he'd set up house in the ashram, an empty
temple, and a tiny unoccupied room with a camp bed
had been made ready for me. There was no electricity
or running water. My host had learnt Hindi. He
explained the complex structure of the village to me,
the castes, the guilds, what some people ate, what
others didn't eat, who was allowed to marry whom,
the tenancy arrangements, the customs, the taboos
and the conflicts. It so happened that the parliamentary elections were taking place. The polling booth
was a tent guarded by armed soldiers. Since hardly
anyone could read or write, the parties used posters
on which their symbols could be seen—an open hand,
an umbrella, a bicycle. The villagers queued up
outside the tent. Young men with moustaches went
on and on at them, appealing for their votes. Once a
person had cast their vote, they were given a stamp
on their hand. No one could explain how the lists of
those entitled to vote were compiled, but there was a
holiday mood and no violence.

In the ashram a widow from the village looked after the lonely researcher from the other end of the world. It was difficult to work out her age. On a spirit stove she prepared vegetarian dishes that she served in a dozen small dishes. I have seldom eaten anything more delicious.

My host had not only abandoned his theories but also the jeans and shirts of his origin and lay in bed, wrapped in a dressing gown. In the evening, he could only get to sleep if his motherly housekeeper told him fairy stories that she narrated in a kind of singsong voice. I had the feeling he was a happy man.

And you?

In March, I was back in Moscow and went to Peredelkino with Masha. Just imagine a summer's day in the country. You're among friends who've known each other for years. No one thinks there's a spy sitting at the table with you.

First the *zakuski*, the hors d'oeuvres—pickled cucumbers, blinis with sour cream, stolichny salad with chicken, hard-boiled eggs, peas, diced potatoes, gherkins and mayonnaise. Vodka with everything. An atmosphere that's totally lacking in New York or Berlin.

Most of those present have been through a lot. Perhaps, old Korney Chukovsky is still there—every

Russian child knows his poems, 'The Telephone', 'The Elephant' and 'The Crocodile'. He must be close to 90. And what about Lydia, his daughter? I haven't read her book. That's no surprise since it was never published during the Soviet era. But, all I need to do is to ask Margarita, she knows about Lydia's friendship with Anna Akhmatova and what she did to save her poems.

In that kitchen they all remember those who were murdered and those who survived. Only a visitor from another world will be unable to understand why some perished and others escaped as if by a miracle. Such as Konstantin Paustovsky, all six volumes of his *Story of a Life* finally managed to get published then. That's the man who claimed he could read the course of world history from the surface of a pavement in Odessa or Leningrad. He's not there sitting at the kitchen table any more because he died in Moscow in 1968, aged 76.

It's ages since you could have got a gathering like that together around a table. But you should beware of nostalgia.

After months of struggle with the bureaucracy, everything was sorted out in Moscow. There was even a flower stall with tulips and carnations. In a state-run clothes-hire shop brides and grooms could hire a white wedding dress and a dark suit for a modest fee. They waited in the vestibule with their families until it was their turn. The registrar was a corpulent woman. The bouquets adorning her office were as voluptuous as she was. Beneath the Soviet flag she droned on about the duties socialism demanded of us. Then, she read out the marriage certificate:

> Enzensberger, Johann Magnus, citizen of the German Federal Republic, born 1929, and Makarova, Maria, daughter of Alexander, citizen of the USSR, born 1943, were married on 20 July 1967; the corresponding entry, no. 5663, was made in the files of the Registry Office on 20 July 1967. Place of registration: Wedding Palace of the Marriage Registry Department of the City of Moscow.

Not long afterwards, following two divorces and one wedding, we could embrace at Zoo Station in West Berlin one Tuesday morning in June 1967. Masha had come from Moscow on the sleeper. We drove to my house in Fregestrasse.

That first day turned into a disaster we took along time to get over. I don't know what my beloved imagined our life together would be like but, whatever she thought, she wasn't prepared for the normality of a life that was determined by my work, close relationships, various friendships and habits. That seemed to surprise and confuse her. Why couldn't I do the same as her—drop everything, as she had, and start from the beginning again with her? Everything she saw seemed foreign to her, not to say, hostile. In Moscow, she had resolved to learn German but she never got beyond a few simple sentences. (My knowledge of Russian wasn't much better; whenever I ventured a sentence in her language, she would laugh at me because she found my stammering embarrassing.)

Masha never uttered a German sentence in Berlin. Naturally my regular visitors couldn't stop themselves from talking the way they usually did and it was impossible to translate everything they said into English for her. And the things they were concerned with were of no interest to Masha.

Her jealousy didn't belong to the erotic sphere, it was aroused by everything—my work, my language, my house, that for her was inhabited by eerie spirits. Instead of starting out on the new life she'd hoped for, she'd ended up stranded on some foreign shore. That was something she wasn't prepared for. As soon as we were alone together in a room there could be nothing else apart from her. I was forced to admit that her obsessive love wasn't far removed from tyranny.

That became apparent with terrifying clarity when Dagrun called to say she was coming around. She was living quite close by, together with my brother Ulrich in Kommune 1. I simply refused to abandon our daughter Tanaquil to the ideological lunatic asylum that was the Kommune. She had kept her room in my house and Dagrun looked after her when I wasn't at home.

Masha froze when the two of them appeared. We had a cup of tea. The 10-year-old child behaved with perfect propriety. She made conversation and tried to mediate, like a diplomat. But her labours were in vain. Hardly had we finished our tea and Dagrun and Tanaquil had left than Masha made a scene that could have come from a play by Strindberg.

Did I intend to continue to receive my first wife in my house as if nothing had happened? She didn't know the expression 'a betrayal of our love' but that's what she meant. She was prepared to accept Tanaquil's presence, though under protest, but she refused to tolerate Dagrun coming to see me. For me that was unthinkable. 'There,' I bawled, 'you're up against a brick wall.' Masha picked up her suitcase and started to go—somewhere, anywhere. I couldn't stop her and got a room for her in a nearby guest house. That, for the time being, was the end of our long-awaited reunion.

However absurd this scene seemed to me, when I think back today, I have to admit that Masha must have suspected something. As it was to prove, it wasn't her who was the waverer but me; for she, the weaker woman, unstable, at risk, was prepared to go to any lengths to get what she wanted. I wasn't. That afternoon was just the beginning of an unequal struggle. Masha desperately sought a way out. She talked to her mother, Margarita, and to her mother's friends in Paris and London, who came to her aid. On the third day she left. Yet, ~~despite~~ that we were both far from giving up.

I suspect you were better off than she was. You had other things to keep you occupied, in line with the age-old saying: a woman has her love, a man has things to do.

I wouldn't subscribe to that, but you're right about one point. I wasn't exactly lonely. I knew a hundred people in Berlin. I used to see my friend Gaston Salvatore, who had come from Santiago de Chile in 1965, every day. Beside that there was my regular work, the periodical I was saddled with. Now and then I even wrote a poem. But otherwise, I was alone at home. Dagrun didn't stick it out in Kommune 1 for long, and Tanaquil had been unhappy with life in Berlin for ages. She was determined to remain Norwegian. So the two of them soon went back to Norway, to the white sea-captain's house on the island, which I was happy to make over to them.

Are you trying to tell me that you stayed away from your home in the north?

No. I went to Oslo at least every six months.

So what did you think you were doing? You'd split up, got a divorce, and despite that you kept shacking up with her again? That shows remarkable chutzpah.

I wasn't the bad father you're trying to present me as. I've always looked after my daughter. If you like, I can show you letters from Tanaquil which prove it. Even my Russian novel didn't separate us.

That sounds like an excuse.

No use crying over spilt milk.

And you weren't concerned about what was going on in Berlin at all?

Oh but I was. The Senate was expecting a state visit from the USA. It was a vice president from South Dakota who was called Hubert Horatio Humphrey, a name that made you think of the hero of Nabokov's novel *Lolita*. The members of Kommune 1 also intended to pay their respects. Together with a dozen others, the usual suspects had discussed in Uwe Johnson's apartment how to receive the guest. Kunzelmann, who always liked to play the crackpot dictator, suggested a smoke-bomb attack. The others thought that was too risky, only Langhans was willing to go along with it. The usual police-spy was there too.

On 4 April the Political Police arrested 11 students, among them Fritz Teufel and Ulrich Enzensberger. The Berlin press, servile and hysterical as it was, ran the following headlines: 'Police Foil Assassination Attempt on Hubert Humphrey! FU Students Made Bombs with Explosives from Peking.' (*Morgenpost*); 'Mao Cocktails Made from Plastic Bags Filled with Highly Explosive Chemicals!' (*Bild*); 'Enzensberger's Son One of the Humphrey Conspirators'. The newspapers got it just about as wrong as they could: the bags the police had taken possession of contained, besides flour and dye, just one powder for making blancmange that became legendary.

The next morning, a long stretch of the Otto-Suhr-Allee was cordoned off. Despite that hundreds of demonstrators had managed to gather outside Charlottenburg Castle and start their favourite chant of 'You-Ess-Ay-Ess-Ay-Ess-Ess.' It was something I simply couldn't miss. But I wasn't arrested, just taken into custody and put in a warm cell in a nearby police station. After having my fingerprints and photograph taken, I quietly fell asleep. The next morning I was released. The members of the Kommune were also set free and immediately held their first press conference.

Even the *New York Times* reported on 6 April: '11 Seized in Berlin in a Reported Plot to Kill Humphrey.' Uwe Johnson was alarmed and asked his friend Gunter Grass to clear 'my former guests Herr Ulrich Enzensberger and Frau Dagrun Enzensberger, as well as all other people living there,' out of his apartment.

That was done and the members of the Kommune moved into an older building on Stuttgarter Platz, right in the middle of the red-light area.

As for myself, none of the many states where I've been on my travels has felt obliged to lock me up, not even the one to which, as my passport says, I belong. A single night behind bars is all I have to show. There can hardly be clearer proof of how harmless I am.

That surprises you?

Yes, but I can understand it and I prefer it like that. What is also striking is that no secret service has ever made any effort to recruit me. Neither the West German BND, nor the East German State Security Service, nor the KGB has ever asked a small favour of me, as was standard during the Cold War, even though I travelled to Moscow and other places so often. Perhaps they knew I would have told everyone about such an approach. Or, they simply thought I wasn't a good source.

So you never made it either as a spy or as a good comrade. What was the reason for that?

I was too often absent, just as I was at school, at university and in the office. During the Shah's visit to Berlin, which was the start of so many things, I was sitting in a kitchen in Moscow. I kept on not being there, or simply still in bed, when there were battles in the streets. I even missed the fight on Tegeler Weg.

Gaston told me about the tear gas, the click-clack, click-clack of the dozens of glass allies and marbles they had in their pockets to roll at the mounted police to frighten their horses.

Once, in Kreuzberg, it was still a working-class district at the time, I stood on the edge of the street watching two plump women on the third floor; they were leaning on cushions at the open window, amazed at the rows of demonstrators, arms linked and chanting at the tops of their voices, 'Ho! Ho! Ho-Chi-Minh!' or 'What do we want? A red West Berlin!' —only a couple of hundred yards from the Wall.

It certainly wasn't sensible.

Who was sensible in those days! That isn't a characteristic I can claim for myself. But, of course, the Kreuzberg women watching the demonstration were absolutely right. The Red Army was a couple of miles away, ready to put an end to West Berlin's existence as an island in the sea of socialism and introduce a system that wouldn't pay any heed to the rowdy mob.

And what did Masha have to say to all that?

She was not amused. I got her next letter a couple of weeks later. She wrote that she intended to spend the summer in Russia: 'Come and see me as soon as you can. You're always welcome at my mother's house.'

And she didn't have to ask you twice.

No. Not long before that Margarita had met a friend from wartime. He was called Igor and I think he was originally an engineer. They had both been evacuated from Moscow and lived beyond the Urals for a few years. They were young and attracted to each other. Then they said goodbye and it seemed as if the affair was over. Twenty-five years later they happened to run into each other in Moscow. The man recognized her immediately, spoke to her and invited her to have a glass of tea. By now he had made a career in the Party and worked in the Central Committee. The two of them found fulfilment after all those years. But Russian novels don't normally have a happy end. When Igor moved in with Margarita, his wife committed suicide and Masha was beside herself with rage when she learnt that her mother had married once again.

I don't understand that.

Masha's jealousy was not at all like the emotion that torments others. We were often separated for months, but she never asked whether I'd been to bed with another woman. Not a word, not a glimmer of suspicion. But when I was with her, it was enough for me to go out to buy the paper, talk in German with a visitor from Germany, to need some peace and quiet in order to write—then she would behave as if I were stabbing her in the back. And her attitude to her mother was exactly the same. Every time she went home she took over the apartment, the dacha and Margarita. And suddenly there was a man she didn't know! How could her mother hurt her feelings like that? It was unpardonable! She never went back to the apartment in Lavrushinsky Street. Only after some time was she prepared to meet her mother in a cafe. She never spoke a single word to her new husband.

Despite that I went back to Moscow because I wanted to see her. Mostly I flew with Aeroflot because it was cheaper. My money was gradually running out. The constant back-and-forth by plane was expensive and the rents, the hotels, the telephone bills were having a big impact on my bank account as well. But the Russian intelligentsia has always despised money. Even back in the days of Alexander Herzen it was looked on as an invention of the petty bourgeoisie to which they felt superior. Perhaps, there was something in that.

A new underground line was being built underneath Margarita's house in Moscow. Every four minutes the glass in her display cabinet would tremble. Masha's mother accepted her daughter's moods with the patience of Job, but I could see she was concerned about the situation. Marina, who always knew what was happening, told me that now anyone who put down 3,000 roubles in cash could escape from the kommunalka. You only needed to get yourself a little flat in a high-rise development outside the city; you then had to pay off the rest over twenty years.

The first swallow of capitalism before the birds of prey appeared over the horizon?

Could be. But Marina knew that to live in those suburbs you had to put up with muddy footpaths to get to the nearest shop, the nearest Metro station. That being the case, she preferred to stay in her little room on Kalinin Prospect, she said.

But she got a refuge for Masha and me on one of those estates. The building still hadn't been finished; you had to traverse a deep puddle to get to the entrance. Like an idiot, I suggested we resort to self-help, negotiate with the neighbours, find a wheelbarrow to fill in the ruts outside the building with soil and steal a plank from some building site. Furious, Masha told me to shut up, because in the first place we were living there illegally, that is without papers, meaning the janitor could inform on us at any time, and secondly because any improvement carried out without permission involved incalculable risks. Only a foreigner like me, she said, could be so stupid as to make such a suggestion.

And Moscow wasn't a solution anyway, neither for me nor for Masha. She preferred living in London most of all. She liked the town. Her English was excellent. She was familiar with the literature. She had friends there. A small flat was found for her in Battersea. So she moved to London and I went to see her there as often as I could. I became a regular customer of British Airways. Our Russian novel c ontinued. Yearning and quarrels, banality and love alternated in a way familiar to any reader of Chekhov. And the scenes we made weren't just half-hour or two-hour matters, they generally continued until we were completely exhausted. I've always been proud of myself for abhorring violence. Despite that I'm surprised I didn't strangle Masha in the grey light of dawn. I came close to it more than once.

What kind of prospects of employment did she see for herself?

Apart from a few Russian lessons for English students, Masha could see nothing for herself in England and things in Moscow didn't look any better.

Now you're acting as if you were just calmly going about your business in Berlin. A bit of editing, a short trip God knows where . . . But there is one episode you'd rather pass over in silence.

What are you talking about?

Wasn't there your performance outside Schöneberg Town Hall?

Now you mention it, yes. I'd just dropped in on my brother and found all the members of Kommune 1 in the best of moods. They were dressing up for the next instalment of their political revue. This time they intended to sabotage a state ceremony—the memorial ceremony for a worthy president of the old Reichstag who had recently died.

One of them had cobbled together a black cardboard coffin with the label: *Senate* in which the patriarch of K. 1, dressed in a nightshirt, was to be taken to the Town Hall. There one of his supporters had to lift up the coffin lid in full view of the gathered TV cameras. Then, Kunzelmann was to rise from the grave and scatter leaflets among the crowd. And that is exactly what happened.

And you went along with this action?

I had no idea who this Paul Löbe was, the man who was to be honoured: a Social Democrat who voted against the Enabling Act in 1933 and who was twice sent to a concentration camp by the Nazis.

And you played a role in this street theatre? And now I suppose you regret it.

If it had been that alone! But there was much worse stuff in the leaflet the members of the Kommune distributed to the public. Even today I've no idea who was responsible for it.

Is that enough for you? I presume you're enjoying sitting back going through the times when I made a fool of myself. That's not only unfair, it's a typical sign of old age. You're no longer capable of doing something really stupid.

Do we really want to discuss the advantages of youth and old age? You can't mean that seriously. Let's get back to your little Russian novel.

You do keep harping on about that, but OK. One fine day I received a registered letter the contents of which completely surprised me. It was from a university somewhere in New England: Wesleyan in Connecticut. It was signed by the president, a man by the name of Victor L. Butterfield, a worthy gentleman who had been in charge of the University since 1943. He was ambitious and had resolved to set up an Institute for Advanced Studies. To which he wanted to appoint me. I never found out what gave him that idea. He offered me a position for a whole academic year and a considerable salary, all completely free of the obligations that are usual for members of a university.

The letter also contained a brochure with photos of idyllic autumnal scenes. The core of the campus consisted of buildings such as you see everywhere in New England: neo-Gothic, neo-Tudor, neo-classical, with turrets and Doric columns, all surrounded by parkland. The sleepy little town in which the *liberal arts* college had been established in the middle of the nineteenth century was called Middletown, a name it entirely lived up to.

'Think over my proposal. The best thing would be for you to visit Wesleyan as soon as you have the time. I have taken the liberty of enclosing an air ticket that you can use at any time.'

If I know you, you flew there while all hell was being let loose in Berlin.

Yes.

Another of your attempts to escape, I suppose.

Call it what you like. But the protest movement was getting under way in New York and California as well. Only not in Middletown. That was an oasis of quiet. Things were very civilized beneath the maple trees. I was reminded of Nabokov's most tender novel, *Pnin*, which is set in such an environment. But at least Wesleyan could point to former members such as Emerson, Martin Luther King and John Cage.

That wasn't your real reason. You just wanted to carry on with your novel.

Yes, I rang Masha at once and told her about the opportunity to start a new chapter—not in Moscow, or in London, never mind Berlin, but in another, neutral setting. Neither for me nor for her were there any

revenants from the past in New England. She immediately declared she was ready to accompany me.

When I explained my personal situation to Mr
Butterfield, he smiled. 'Your wife will not have the
least difficulty here. Our Russian Department will be
delighted. And a comfortable house will be at your
disposal as well as an office with secretary of your
own.'

*And all that just as the Vietnam War was reaching its
climax.*

'Dissent and protest,' the president went on, 'are
nothing unusual over here. It's part of our tradition.'

You accepted, of course.

Not immediately. There was something else, you see.
In the autumn of 1967 there was a poetry festival in
London, in a new huge, bunker-like building by the
Thames. Like the gentlemen that they were, W. H.
Auden and William Empson stayed in the background. The star of the evening was Pablo Neruda. I
knew almost everything he'd written and I liked his
early poems 'Las furias y las penas' and those in
Residencia en la tierra so much that at some point I'd
translated them into German with the help of some
Chilean friends. He knew his own poems by heart and
loved reciting them, with priest-like deliberation, in a
loud, booming voice, almost choked with tears—just
the way Russian poets traditionally read their works.

After our performance at the Queen Elizabeth Hall all the participants were invited to a party on a houseboat on the Thames. The Finnish and Serbo-Croat writers were there as well, wolfing down the Irish stew and drinking for all they were worth.

I don't know when Neruda was born. He'd claimed it was his birthday, but he did that quite often; he had no objection to being the focus of attention.

After a while someone asked where the guest of honour was. Only after an extensive search was he found in a dark corner at the stern, a radio pressed to his ear. He'd been waiting for the announcement from Stockholm. It had come, however it didn't concern him but Miguel Asturias, a novelist who not only came from South America but was a Guatamalan into the bargain. Every Chilean was bound to take that as an insult, but what was much worse that in so doing the members of the Swedish Academy had exhausted their Ibero-American quota for a long time. Everyone tried to comfort the poet but eventually a doctor had to be called to treat Neruda who had fallen unconscious. That put a real damper on the party mood and we all took our coats and went home.

———

What's the point of that story? It has nothing to do with you, with Masha or with your plans?

That may be so. You'd like everything neat and tidy, like an accountant. But that wasn't the way it was. However, if you insist. We arrived in Connecticut in October 1967. I've got that in writing. She came from Moscow, I from Berlin and we boarded a transatlantic steamer in Bremen. In the evening, there was dancing in the first class, the band played old Glenn Miller standards and there was a gigolo there for the brewery owners' widows from Minneapolis. On the second day of the crossing we heard on the radio of the death of Che Guevara in Bolivia.

Hardly had we arrived in Middletown than the first demonstrators were rolling up outside the Pentagon. Not in their hundreds and thousands, as they did later, but the unrest was increasing in some universities. Not in Middletown, though. Apart from the main street, where there were liquor stores and cash dispensers, a diner and an estate agent, the town was deserted at night. Our address was: Home Avenue. Our villa had 14 rooms, three bathrooms and three garages, a front garden and a veranda. Our predecessor there was a political scientist who wrote speeches for the president of the United States. I was allowed to use his study, which they called his *den*, and was on a kind of mezzanine floor. We could eat à la carte in the Faculty Club as often as we liked and there were delightful invitations to the homes of the professors.

We managed to stick it out in Middletown for four months. Coming from Berlin, I wasn't used to the total calm at the high point of the war. What business did I have in that idyll? It was too good to be true. And Masha wasn't happy in Middletown either. She couldn't get on with her work.

What work?

She wanted to write something about the Russian avant-garde of the 1920s. More she wouldn't say.

Was there anywhere at all where she'd fit in? Both Berlin and Moscow were out of the question for her.

Masha was a *displaced person*. But one who lived in a padded paradise. She didn't like it in USA and a new round of our quarrels began. On a dull January day, in 1968, a letter with a Cuban stamp arrived. It was from a ministry in Havana.

————

Another of these messages out of the blue! First it was the mysterious Signor Vigorelli who sent you off to Leningrad; then, as you claim, there came an invitation to Moscow and Baku that led to a Russian novel, and now you're telling us there was an inexplicable letter from Cuba.

Believe it or not, it was pure chance.

What did this incredible letter say?

It was an invitation to a cultural congress. The topic was so banal that I immediately forgot it. I knew from experience that as a guest at a festival or as a member of a delegation you understood next to nothing. But my curiosity was roused and Masha insisted on accompanying me.

You accepted, of course?

What's that grin supposed to mean? The journey there was complicated. There were no flights from New York to Cuba, the USA government had imposed a trade embargo. You had to get a visa in Mexico. From there, there was just one connection to the island on an old Ilyushin plane of Cubana de Aviación.

And what were the pair of you after? The ultimate left-wing utopia?

In Villa San Cristóbal de La Habana—as the city has been called since it was founded in 1519—the mood was exuberant, euphoric, the atmospheric pressure quite different from that in Moscow, East Berlin or Warsaw. That was very attractive. At least, the Cuban revolution hadn't been imported on Soviet tanks. It had been achieved independently of the Russians. I had the impression that the majority of the people in the streets didn't just accept it, they were happy about it.

Castro had invited no fewer than 500 authors, scientists and artists. Some had been refused a passport or exit visa by their own government. Sartre was ill and sent his apologies but otherwise all the old acquaintances from the European Left met in the Habana Libre, that used to be the Hilton: Eric Hobsbawm, Michel Leiris, Luigi Nono, Julio Cortázar, the publishers Giulio Einaudi and Giangiacomo Feltrinelli. It wasn't that the debates brought much that was new to light. The faithful from the Eastern Block parroted the Party line and the Chinese hadn't turned up at all. But a touch of controversy was not just permitted, it was even desired.

The French caused a minor brouhaha when the painter David Siqueiros appeared at the opening of an exhibition. An old Stalinist, he'd attacked Trotsky's house in Mexico with machine guns. He intended to kill him, but Trotsky survived. Although Siqueiros later expressed his regret for the assassination attempt, the *Quartier Latin* was determined to extract revenge. A Surrealist lady poet gave him a kick in the backside and shouted, 'Best wishes from André Breton.'

People in Havana had other things to occupy them. They danced to the rumba beat on the Rampa or headed off to a baseball match. Castro played simultaneous chess on 10 boards and got annoyed when he was beaten. Everyone was celebrating a political carnival.

Look what I've got here.

A few old illustrated magazines.

That's three substantial special issues of *Bohemia* that a pedlar offered me on just the second day I was there—waste paper from 1985/59. I immediately bought them. *Bohemia*—God knows where they got that title—is a traditional periodical, founded in 1908, I believe, and still going strong. The older numbers made fascinating reading, reporting on the first phase of the revolution after it was victorious, when the myth of the *barbudos* still lacked any real political content.

At that time the country must have been in a fever of relief, such as there was in 1945 when the war was over in Germany and the Americans were determined not to exact revenge. (The rule of the exiled dictator Batista has repeatedly been compared to the Nazi regime by over-eager journalists.)

Pictured in the magazine were not only Castro— at that time still with 'Dr' and spectacles—together with a youthful Che Guevara, posing right next to them were the middle-class opposition politicians who had returned from exile.

Lovers of statistics maintain that prior to 1959, Cuba was one of the richest countries in South America; that the standard of living was as high as in Spain or Chile and that 80 per cent of Cubans could read and write. But who believes these figures!

There are always people who don't appear in official calculations.

Further on in *Bohemia* there are photos of tortured bodies covered in stab wounds. On the next page, a report describes recent executions with almost sadistic relish. The worst pictures, however, worse than the mutilated corpses, come from the Mazorra, a Cuban lunatic asylum—naked children, half starved on rusty bedsteads, sick people squatting crammed together in the courtyard, the so-called dog kennels, and an old woman, half witch, half prophetess, naked, with huge eyes and mouth wide open. If it's true that lunatics are the hidden truth of a society . . .

Another report, almost over-optimistic, tells of the destruction of the casinos and betting shops: the gaming machines dragged out into the street by the crowd, the roulette tables overturned and set on fire, just as the Spanish anarchists did in the past. It was a symbolic action. Just as the members of the Paris Commune shot at clock towers in order to gain time.

Untouched by all that, in 1959, the advertising industry continued its campaigns for Pan Am, Esso, Lucky Strike and Alcoa together with small ads praising uplift bras, patent medicines and dubious private schools. A cardinal gave a brand of soap the apostolic blessing and had himself photographed doing so.

The leading article of 11 January has the headline 'Against Communism' and quotes a speech by Fidel Castro: 'The government will terminate all treaties with states that use dictatorial measures, in the first instance that concerns the Soviet Union. It has suppressed freedom in a dozen European countries and used machine guns to fire on the defenceless people of Hungary. There is no greater example of despotism in the world.'

These old newspapers give a snapshot of the time. The revolution is in the balance, at its most dangerous moment. The mixture of mutiny and marketing—Guevara on the left and Brilliantine on the right—that was normal at the time but is disturbing today.

Incidentally, the pages of *Bohemia* are thronged with pictures of people who have disappeared: renegades, outcasts and the dead. What becomes clear from them is that without the stupidity and greed of the Americans, this revolution would have sunk without trace, like a dozen others in Latin America, survived by the sweet Coca Cola girl telling all those who dream of revolution, 'Have a break.'

————

OK. Except that unfortunately your waste paper doesn't tell us what all that has to do with the pair of you.

Nothing.

What were your plans?

The Cubans maintained that people such as us were urgently needed as *tecnicos extranjeros*—foreign technicians. One of the olive-green *comandantes* asked me whether we would like to stay for some time in Cuba. He couldn't say what the technical matters were in our case.

I at least saw this invitation as an opportunity for the two of us, perhaps, our last. Neither of us knew the island. It was virgin territory. No distractions from the past, no language that only one of us could speak, no family complications. Moreover both of us spoke reasonably good Spanish. Wasn't that worth a try?

A pretty unpolitical speech for the defence! You just wanted to get away from Middletown, you and your Russian woman. Making a splash at the same time.

There was no other way about it. The only antidote to all the goodwill and hospitality was international politics.

Didn't they treat you well in New England? They'd offered you refuge for a whole year, a fellowship, a pile of money, a much too big house and an air-conditioned office with a secretary who had nothing to do. Others would have considered themselves fortunate. But you two were ungrateful. A golden cage, you muttered, complained about a war on the other side of the world, snubbed your benefactors and set off a public scandal that even made it to the front page of the New York Times.

Originally that wasn't an open letter. Since the good Mr Butterfield had retired, I had to approach his successor, Edwin Etherington, to take my leave. To cap it all, he was also the chairman of the New York Stock Exchange. Should I read my letter out to you?

No. I know what's in it. 'Why I Left America', you proclaimed.

I thought Mr Etherington would silently note what I'd written and let us go. But then a busybody professor, who assumed he was on my side, leaked the letter to the press.

Not what you'd call elegant! One embarrassment after the other. Uwe Johnson really rubbed your nose in it in his Anniversaries. *To show his disapproval, he calls you Herr Enzensberger in the book. He didn't like you going to Cuba either.*

Johnson was malicious but he wasn't wrong in all respects, I have to give him that. What he failed to see was the unintentionally comic side of our Cuban adventure.

At least I did have some idea of how I might make myself useful in Cuba. The young diplomats Castro dispatched to London, Berlin or Stockholm were totally out of their depth. I knew that. They had no idea how things were in capitalism. The old hands of the diplomatic service, who had a better idea, had escaped to Miami in time. A little six-month seminar to teach the young mulattos from the Sierra the basics was what I had in mind. A little history, minimal knowledge of the basic law or the constitution, of parties, unions, parliaments and law courts. What I wanted to drill into them was that you have to know whom you're dealing with: ministers and the media, lobbyists and civil servants, from regional authorities all the way to Brussels. It couldn't do any harm to tell them something about that, I thought.

Great! They said in Havana. Agreed! Come back in autumn. By then we'll have everything arranged for you and your wife.

For Masha, that would mean waiting in London or Moscow, and for me, a return to the turbulence of Berlin, to the trench warfare, to the chaos. I felt like a billiard ball being knocked around the table. But, there was a third player involved in this game of cannons whom I happened to meet in the hotel foyer.

There I was introduced to Prince Sihanouk, who had come from Cambodia for negotiations in Havana, and his son, who looked like a well-brought-up grammar school boy. He was wearing an elegant greyish-blue Mao suit, made to measure, and while we were sitting in the lobby the ambassador, who was accompanying him, suddenly said, 'We'd be delighted if you were to come and join us in Phnom Penh. I'd be happy to see to the air ticket and a visa and have a limousine waiting for you at the airport.'

Just a minute! First things first. Stick to the order in which they happened.

You'd like that, wouldn't you, but that's not the way things are. You can forget chronology. You like to point out that in thermodynamics turbulence can't be described with linear equations. Or, if you prefer, at least think of Brownian molecular motion. Just as every particle suspended in a heated gas is subject to random, uncontrollable fluctuations, exactly the same is true of the political, erotic, climatic and, damn it all, moral turbulence we are dealing with here.

Just imagine you're sitting for hours in your dark editing room looking through the material your memory supplies—here a take, there a whole sequence, and in between black film. That's nothing for a nit-picker like you. It's pointless trying to put those fragments in order. They'll never make a documentary.

Moreover, my dear chap, you've probably forgotten how loud the tumult was. Even just the music, there was no escape from it. An overwhelming feast of sound: rumba on the Rampa, jazz in New York, a military band playing 'Black Eyes'—an old Russian evergreen—in the Moscow Park of Achievements.

The Stones' latest record roared into our pituitary glands: 'Let It Bleed'. Muzak in the hotel toilets: 'Guantanamera', 'And the shark has pretty teeth, dear'. A deafening cacophony in the Electric Circus, compressed-air hammers and whistle sounds in the Week of the Latest Music. The German hits alone continued to soothe the ear with their schmaltzy tones.

The 'Song of the United Front' on vinyl, and in Palo Alto, sung by a tinny computer voice: 'Daisy, Daisy, give me you answer, do! / I'm half crazy, all for the love of you! / It won't be a stylish marriage. / I can't afford a carriage, / But you'll look sweet / Upon the seat / Of a bicycle made for two'—Copyright IBM. I have to admit that when I heard it I didn't think of the Countess of Warwick, but of Masha.

———

Despite all that, you went along with everything the little prince proposed on the spur of the moment in a hotel foyer in Havana.

Yes. I liked the idea of disappearing without leaving a forwarding address. To go off like an embezzler with his creditors and the bailiffs after him.

I think your journey around the world was nothing but an escape. Even though Interpol has never shown an interest in you and no state prosecutor has ever issued a warrant for your arrest.

That is true.

Perhaps you were running away from your wife.

Do you have to be right all the time? I grasped the chance of thinking about something other than the chaos in Berlin, my Russian novel, the Cuban revolution, my generous publisher Siegfried Unseld and the house in Norway that was no longer my home.

I set off on a blind flight lasting several months. In my jacket pocket were forms with red carbon copies filled out by hand and stapled together so that they could folded out to make a paper chain. They were my tickets.

Now we're in a different film again.

Nonsense. There was no screenplay. My next stop was San Francisco. Columbia Avenue, on the corner of Broadway, between Chinatown and North Beach. I knew the poets of City Lights Books, you see. I just walked straight into the house with the clerestory windows. Lawrence Ferlinghetti gave me a fraternal 'Hi' and a ginger ale. Gregory Corso was there as well. I knew a few lines from his leaflet BOMB:

> . . . O Bomb I love you
> I want to kiss your clank eat your boom
> You are a paean an acme of scream
> a lyric hat of Mister Thunder

O resound thy tanky knees
BOOM BOOM BOOM BOOM BOOM
. . .
Yes Yes into our midst a bomb will fall . . .

I'd already translated something by him:

The Last Gangster

Waiting by the window
my feet enwrapped with the dead boot-
    leggers of Chicago
I am the last gangster, safe, at last,
waiting by a bullet-proof window

I look down the street and know
The two torpedoes from St Louis.
I've watched them grow old
. . . guns rusting in their arthritic hands

At that time he was 38 but, with his troglodyte fore-
head and glowing eyes, he looked much older, like his
last gangster.

———

And what was the next sequence in your private cinema?

San Diego.

Tell me why you went there.

That metropolis of the armament moguls, surfers and the Marines is pretty unattractive but it was there of all places, at the University of California, that Herbert Marcuse, an old hand from the New York Institute for Social Research and the OSS intelligence agency during the Second World War, had come as professor of political science in 1964. We knew each other from Berlin, of course, where he also taught at the University and where his appearances were a sensational success. And Reinhard Lettau, an old but not very close friend, had also taken a teaching post in San Diego, and in a subject he knew very well— German studies.

We sat by the swimming pool, drank a sundowner and argued about one-dimensional man that the philosopher had once invented. (Presumably a man squashed flat was what he had in mind, but that would have been two-dimensional. Geometry was never his strong point.)

Both of them were heavily engaged in the rebellion against the war in Vietnam. Lettau's teaching duties hardly suffered from that. He told me that for some considerable time now he had only dealt with two works of German literature for his students: *Heinrich von Ofterdingen* by the Romantic poet Novalis, and Kafka's stories. How I enjoyed the contradictions between these two, their seriousness just as much as their quirks.

Then on to Papeete, the capital of French Polynesia. The tricolour was flying over the official residence of the prefect. Tahiti was France's outpost in the Pacific. Groups of tourists from Japan and the USA were being offloaded at the airport and since I didn't want to get on the waiting buses, I had to haggle with an illegal taxi driver to avoid the crush. The driver, a stocky Polynesian who only spoke broken French, took me by a circuitous route to a dilapidated wooden colonial building at the end of an avenue of palms. There was a cloudburst with torrential rain pouring on the straw roof.

In my memory the camera pans towards an open veranda. You can hear the rain drumming on the roof. Eight muscular Indios are sitting in wobbly chairs, smoking and drowsily staring into space. They can neither read nor write and they've no idea how they came to end up on Tahiti. A formally dressed gentleman with a melancholy expression, who greets me politely, explains that they're waiting for money, papers, assurances and a plane that's to take them to Paris. I introduce myself to the gentleman and he hands me his visiting card. He's called Salvador Allende and is a senator. Hardly anyone outside Chile has heard of him. The men he's taken charge of are the last survivors of Che Guevara's Bolivian expedition. In the morning, he takes me back to the capital, where he has a telephone call to make, and I continue my blind flight westward.

———

On the other side of the world, there was one more of your all-too-many literature festivals.

You mean the Writers' Week in Adelaide, South Australia? Actually it was nothing to do with me, I just happened to be in the vicinity. I assume that, just as in Moscow or London, there were speeches of welcome which I can't remember. Poets took the stage, declaiming lines in barely comprehensible languages, and after the book-signing hour went on to a boozy party.

That wasn't what has left some trace in my memory, but a sheep farm in the outback, far away from the city, only accessible by dusty roads. The name I remember clearly: Anlaby, Bagot Well. The owner was called Geoffrey Dutton, a gentleman, author, horseman and war pilot. I still have a few film sequences of him.

What do I see on his desk? A signed photograph of Queen Victoria. In the barn, he shows me a magnificent motor car from the 1930s in which he once crossed the whole of the continent as far as the Timor Sea, over the rough ground, for there were no proper tracks in those days.

Then the opal mine in Coober Pedy, that naturally has nothing to do with the remarkable Mr Dutton and his beautiful daughters. It is said that in the language of the aboriginals the name of this desolate place means 'White Man in a Hole'. And indeed, in 60-foot deep shafts which they've dug themselves, a hundred bearded men with picks, spades and miners' lamps are churning up the red soil in the search for a few stones that agents from Sydney will relieve them of for a few coppers and a bottle of whisky. Who or what took me to that arid place, 400 miles to the north of Adelaide? Why go all that way? When I rummage around in the bottom drawer of my desk I find a few opals I'd forgotten, a harlequin, a milky cabochon and three shimmering, deep-red and emerald-green triplets that can only have cost a few dollars. Since the days of classical antiquity the opal has been considered the talisman of thieves and spies.

From there on it was only possible to proceed by the *milk run*. That is a small, single-engine aeroplane, used to deliver the post and goods to remote places in the outback. Each trip takes the pilot three days to cross the continent.

How did you get him to take you? You were the only passenger. What did the farmers tell you? Did you get a friendly welcome? Why did they feed you? What had you to offer them? Did the little monoplane ever break down?

Where did it refuel? In Alice Springs? Didn't you ever talk to an Aborigine?

All I can remember is that the pilot, a short, stocky Welshman, with whom I hitch-hiked to the north coast, dropped me off in Port Darwin on a boiling-hot day. What was the point of going there? Always the same question, to which I have no answer. In the hut, where sleepy Englishmen were waiting for a flight, I drank a couple of bottles of James Squire's Nine Tales with a little layabout, whom I treated to a round.

In Singapore, before the head of state allowed the excavators to clear away the old alleyways of the town centre, you could eat well for next to nothing in the steaming hot-food stalls by the side of the street; while in the Raffles, a rather run-down remnant of the British Empire that didn't live up to its reputation, the tourists knocked back their Singapore slings. In Bangkok, the GIs didn't bother to go and see the pagodas but used their short leave to recover from the exertions of war in specialized brothels: *Wee speek Inglish!*

———

I've been in the no-man's-land of too many airports. Long, glittering walkways past superfluous shops, elsewhere draughty shacks, jam-packed buses, endless queues. Those familiar with underdevelopment can gauge the degree from the time lapse between the check-in at the desk and departure. It can be up to three hours. Crackling loudspeakers announce delays in the local dialect. To pass the time there are surly customs officers there who rummage through cases and bundles until, with a gesture of triumph, they take a forbidden sausage away from a helpless old woman or a bottle of whisky from an unbeliever. The more thugs in uniform there are standing around in the hall clutching their machine pistols, the stronger the sweaty stench of military dictatorship.

But you never paid for your air tickets.

No, I didn't. That was Prince Sihanouk or his son, the grammar-school pupil in a Mao suit. In Phnom Penh, I was picked up by a chauffeur in livery and taken to a huge apartment, all in the French taste, neo–Louis Seize. A garden party in the evening with colourful Chinese lanterns and butterflies fluttering around. There was no audience, that would be going too far, but the monarch made himself free to talk to me for a few minutes. He explained everything to me, the Ho Chi Minh Trail, the difficulties with the Vietnamese, the Americans and the Chinese, and why it was important to preserve the neutrality of Cambodia at all cost.

We talked about his opponent, Henry Kissinger, whom I happened to know. I'd met him at my publisher's house. At that time, he'd insisted on speaking

American English with an incredible accent that seemed familiar to me. I asked him if he came from Fürth, a town close to Nuremberg. 'How do you come to know that?'—'I deduced it from your accent.' He didn't like that. At the time of the Indo-China War, he was one of our bêtes noires. 'Perhaps you think I'm a war criminal?' he asked me. And with that he'd hit the nail on the head, for he was without doubt responsible for the extension of the war to Cambodia.

The impression Sihanouk made was quite different from that of his opponent. He was short, possessed excellent French manners and a certain melancholy air. 'Right,' he said to me, 'I'm the head of state, but what does that mean? I'm here to save a country that has no friends.' Actually, he went on, there was no hope of that; he was fighting a losing battle. He was an exile in his own country: that was the subtext of what he was telling me. Later, one of the temple dancers who lived in the palace appeared —a present, like putting flowers in a guest's room. As a gesture, that was all, no one insisted the barbarian from the West should make use of the offer.

I can also remember the people out for peaceful Sunday walks in the ruins of Angkor Wat. They would picnic in the temple city in the jungle, that looks like a forest of stone, and contemplate the hundreds of complicated erotic embraces from the fourteenth century, although the rampant tropical vegetation had long since smothered the pairs of lovers.

Before I left Phnom Penh, I was walking past a miserable street market when I saw an old beggar woman sitting by the entrance to a brothel and got rid of a couple of dollar notes I found in my trousers pocket.

———

You'd lost interest in what was going on in Berlin.

No I hadn't. In February 1968, 3,000 people gathered in the main lecture theatre of the Technical University for an international Vietnam Congress at which Rudi Dutschke, Gaston Salvatore, Peter Weiss and Erich Fried spoke. Once more I was somewhere else, in Berkeley in California. There were all sorts of things going on there too. One year later Nixon came to Berlin. I don't know what happened then.

Didn't you sometimes ask yourself whether the 'movement' had only just begun or whether it was already all over? Perhaps it only existed as its own revenant, just as every fashion gives rise to a retro-look?

I no more managed to get by without thoughts like that than you do. I was the poor comrade who never became a full member, whether we're talking about the Socialist Students' Federation, a flat-share, a commune, the Writers' Association or one of the countless communist parties. I'm not to be seen in the famous photos of demonstrations or street battles. I preferred to remain in the wings.

Yes, my large study was used by the leaders of the various political groups to haggle over money and tactical alliances under the Bomber Command's large map of the world that I'd pinned to the wall. Rudi Dutschke was there, beside him my friend Gaston Salvatore, people such as Bernd Rabehl, Christian Semler and Tilman Fichter from the Socialist Students' Federation, but also less trustworthy figures such as Kunzelmann and Mahler.

Rudi Dutschke was not only a very German phenomenon, he was one that was unimaginable in the west of the country. He was, in fact, the only political leader the opposition to the system produced. Industrious and unwavering as he was, he totally lacked the cynicism without which neither a Trotsky nor a Lenin would have come anywhere near their goals. That was his most vulnerable spot, his Achilles' heel at which not only his opponents could aim but also others who, like the backbenchers in the parliamentary parties, aspired to leading positions. Dutschke was above all that, the idea of making a career for himself was completely alien to him. That made him unassailable and gave him a unique kind of authority. He wasn't suited to be the leader of some deviant sect even though he combined politics and morality with a religious background that the others didn't have.

I did have difficulty with the peculiar language he used. He'd cobbled together a private Marxism that had little in common with the collective academic Marxism of the others. Sometimes I just couldn't understand what he was getting at.

It is impossible to imagine a greater contrast to him than Gaston Salvatore. He always trailed a string of legends behind him—notorious as an unwitting seducer, a drug addict, a behind-the-scenes operator, or famous as an assistant to Antonioni in Rome or a future Chilean ambassador to Peking. With his background he was conversant with the habits of the Latin American oligarchy but often without a penny to his name; full of immense projects, an outright enemy of coercion, moody, vain, generous and ever-ready to help. His drafts for dramas showed great boldness. Many people in Germany found a person such as him provoking; in our country he was envied and hounded at the same time.

Bahman Nirumand was also often there. He was a Persian who had been living in Germany again since 1965 and our friendship went back a long way. I had got to know him in Teheran, during the time of the Shah's rule, at the Goethe Institute that provided a platform for oppositional thinkers. Back then, this thin man with the gold-rimmed spectacles, who looked like a junior teacher, came up and addressed me in faultless, well-articulated German. He it is whom I have to thank for everything I know about Iran. Some years later Bahman's book, *Iran: The New Imperialism in Action*, played a key role, and not only during the Shah's visit to Berlin and its consequences.

Once Peter Schneider was there as well. Dutschke went on at him for so long that he eventually agreed to organize a campaign against the Springer Verlag. To me he didn't seem exactly enthusiastic about such a demand but he agreed to do it. The plan was to follow the London example of the Russell Tribunal and publicly examine the evidence against the Berlin gutter press for inciting its readers to violence against left-wing activists. The tribunal was to proceed according to the standard rules of the administration of justice—there had to be counsels for the prosecution and defence, experts and witnesses. Peter Schneider made a real effort to set up such proceedings. But many of the comrades didn't like the idea, they had different campaigns in mind and dreamt of sabotage and Molotov cocktails, while there were others who were looking for money from competing newspaper publishers or help from East Berlin. As expected, the project fizzled out after the usual squabbles.

I was quite happy to make my house available as a meeting place, but avoided taking part in the struggles between the various groups. The French word for the ambiguous attitude I showed in this is *mauvaise foi*—literally, bad faith. Ethnologists prefer to talk about 'participating observation' when they eat, dance or go to bed with the native population. That seldom produces good results for there's no clear solution to their research problems in prospect. Either they fall prey to the object of their research—in the researchers' jargon that is called *going native*—or, as Margaret Mead did, they invent a legend that they like better than the reality.

————

What the hell made you lead this double life?

I can't even explain that to myself, never mind to you. I suppose I thought it would be a mistake to miss out on an opportunity that's pretty rare in German society. It hadn't happened very often that, as in 1848 or 1919, a minority became active and undermined the prevailing conditions. Even if, as in this case, it was only a pale reflection of earlier struggles, its legacy was a kind of street theatre—at least that was better than nothing.

Naturally the more intelligent of the leaders among the politically aware sensed that they couldn't rely on a writer, however much he liked to spout political slogans. In my case, that was suggested by the energy I put into continuing to work surreptitiously on many things that only appeared years later, or not at all.

So you cheated?

Of course. Are you trying to play the authentic, upright, honest man? That doesn't suit you. It's easy being wise after the event. But by then you've long since forgotten what things were like at the time.

Too true.

———

Once Bahman pulled off a surprise coup in Munich. Together with 65 followers, all wearing black hoods, he occupied the Persian Consulate. They started a hunger strike, the secret service files were seized, and all that with maximum publicity—the television and the press were there, though not the police. When the Police President rang the Consul, it was Nirumand who was on the line, and he very politely but firmly refused the offer of assistance.

Meanwhile, the left-wing groups in Munich—there were eight of them—had also become active. They wanted to issue a leaflet calling for a solidarity demonstration. After 10 hours of negotiations, their 'spokespersons' explained that unfortunately there were 'insurmountable ideological differences of opinion'. Nirumand said, 'Then I'll just have to write the leaflet myself.' It only took him 15 minutes. The eight spokespersons went into the consulate, one after the other, and all found the text excellent. Without Bahman's intervention they would have gone on arguing for ever, 'in order to continue to drive the necessary process of splitting into factions forward.'

There was another Gordian knot that was less easy to cut. Nirumand could do nothing about what was happening in Tehran after the Shah had been driven out. He had to flee the regime of the mullahs himself. Any political action produces unforeseeable consequences. Sometimes it even brings about the opposite of what was intended and success turns into disaster. Even a perceptive man such as my friend couldn't do anything about that.

———

You're digressing again. Were you actually there?

No.

So that has nothing to do with you. Go on with your own story instead. At some time or other Masha and you arrived in Cuba. You wanted to make yourselves useful as technicos extranjeros, didn't you? What came of your good intentions?

Nothing. Every time I called the minister of education, a certain Llanusa, whose responsibility it was, his reply was brief. All he said was, *mañana*, and obviously didn't dream of keeping his promise.

Embarrassing for you.

Not only for me. The people who'd invited us had egg on their faces as well. But we could live with that.

Can you be more precise?

To calm me down the minister suggested a tour around the whole country. That, he said, would make it easier for Masha and me to understand the situation, for it wasn't enough just to know the capital. The suggestion had a familiar ring to it, reminded me of how the people in Moscow had sent me to the most distant corners of the Soviet Union.

We thanked him but told him we didn't think much of the usual sightseeing and wouldn't be happy to be on one of the buses in which foreign delegations were carted around. We would prefer a tour with a chauffeur. He'd see to it, the old fox assured us, and this time Llanusa did keep his promise. We were given a driver of our own, who was called Toni and was both a minder and a black marketeer—a subtropical combination that isn't unusual in Cuba. He had a decrepit Chevrolet in which he drove us wherever we wanted.

Here, though, we didn't have an escort such as Kostya or Marina. Our Toni was too lazy and venal to write reports on Masha and me that no one would read anyway. Nor did I feel any desire to keep a diary, as I'd done in Russia. Therefore all that remains in my memory of our three-week-long trip are a few hastily assembled, jerky film sequences.

First, we went to Pinar del Río, a town surrounded by pine forests in the north-west of the island. It looks a sleepy place but connoisseurs all over the world appreciate what is cultivated and processed in this green province—the best Cuban tobacco. That the women who roll the cigars in the famous factory roll the dark wrappers on their bare thighs is a myth. They work very chastely on piece rates at a long table while the reader at the lectern reads out one of the edifying speeches of the revolutionary José Martí. On the bands and labels are the names of long departed patron saints: Henry Clay, Herman Upmann, and Winston Churchill.

We once made it to a godforsaken place in the mountains at the other end of the island, not far from Baracoa, where in the evening the inhabitants had gathered round a white cloth hung up between two trees. There was a projector on a truck. These people were seeing a film for the first time. As in the days of the Lumière brothers, they sat there spellbound, screaming when a train came hurtling towards them. Who could have set up this expedition to the back-country? It must have been Alfredo Guevara, the founder of the celebrated film institute in Havana.

Fortunately, our chauffeur wasn't interested in the government's cult of relics, so we were spared visits to many of the memorials. In Santiago de Cuba we declined a visit to the Moncada Barracks that has been turned into a museum of the revolution. We preferred to see the fence on Guantánamo, behind which the hated US Navy had made itself at home; a terrible nickel mine; the wedding-cake architecture of Cienfuegos or the caves and tree ferns of the Sierra del Escambray—too much all at once, too much of a rush to write down everything there was to see.

Only after our return, during the boring hours in our hotel, did I find time to write some notes on our last stop:

Trinidad, between the sea and Escambray, one of the oldest towns in Cuba, 30,000 inhabitants, no harbour, no industry, is just a film set. The palaces of the aristocratic families that bear old Spanish names and are too proud to show their coats of arms, are falling into ruin along the streets where grass is growing over the cobblestones. Magnificent pieces of furniture can be made out behind clouded windows. There's hardly any street lighting in Trinidad in the evening. A mulatto child on a dapple-grey horse gallops across the deserted square.

It's only when one of the old noblemen dies that partitions are brought into the palace, washing hung up, a transistor radio blares and children swarm through the portal with the paint peeling off. Some corners of the town have a kind of mummified beauty.

For years the Sierra del Escambray was the centre of an armed uprising against the revolutionary government. The aristocracy, whose delusory pride forbade them to take any political action, was never involved in it.

The palace of the city historian and judge, who is descended from counts, now has a sign that says it is the seat of the 'Committee for the Defence of the Revolution'. His fellow nobles cut him. With a laugh he tells the story of the son of a petty bourgeois from the neighbourhood:

Years after the revolution P., who's a homosexual, developed an enthusiasm for England. He admired Churchill and always sent a long telegram to London on the occasion of the Queen's birthday. He founded an 'English Club' in which British cakes and teas alone were served. At Christmas, he sent out invitations on deckle-edge paper to a meal with Christmas pudding at which dinner jackets were de rigueur.

When he attracted young people of the same background from Camagüey and Havana, he was arrested with five others and sent to a farm for six months to work as an agricultural labourer; the others got off with house arrest. During the trial, he had to admit in public that he was not of noble descent. That was his worst punishment, for the people in the town had become accustomed to call him *el Conde*. His banishment to the country was the only time in his life when he worked. After his release he became involved in the black market, planned to buy a title of nobility in Europe, attempted to escape by boat but failed and was arrested again. Like the

town from which he comes, this poor devil bears all
the stigmata of underdevelopment.

———

*Always these digressions. Tell me, instead, how the pair of
you felt as idle beneficiaries of the revolution.*

As always you're being unfair, old chap. I did what I
could. Naturally I was furious that the job they'd
promised me didn't exist. 'Why on earth did you
bring me here?' I shouted. 'I'm sitting in this hotel,
letting you feed me. What's the point?'—'Oh,' the
officials said, 'the project's fallen through because the
foreign ministry had reservations, but we'll find
something for you.'

So after that I struggled through as an adviser for
the publishing house, as a translator and go-between.
The problem was that in Havana, just as in Moscow,
there were no free apartments, so they had to put us
up in a hotel willy-nilly. As it said in the travel guides,
the Nacional was the best hotel in town. In the past,
the mafia used to book whole suites of rooms. The
gangsters, whether Lucky Luciano or Meyer Lansky,
stayed there, just as the senators, with the striptease
girls in their lap, and the Hollywood stars. Errol Flynn
and Marlene Dietrich were regulars, as was the
unavoidable Hemingway. On the garden terrace, with
the view over the Malecón, Machado's and Batista's
ministers and senators did their business and had

mojitos and daiquiris served. This idyll came to an abrupt end in 1959.

Now we were sitting at the table with a failed guerrillero and with an old Parisian Trotskyist who, in his pleasantly subversive way, peppered us with pellets of bread and quotations from Engels and Freud. There was an American in the uniform of the New Left there as well, who looked like a little Allen Ginsberg. I also remember a Yugoslav arms dealer, a fisherman with his wife on their honeymoon and a Soviet nuclear power engineer. We had a large room with a bathroom. Compared with the situation of normal Cubans, we were living like millionaires.

The old waiters were still there. They had been forbidden to accept tips. But they served us in white tie and tails, as if nothing had happened and the weary pianist continued to play American evergreens that he knew by heart: 'You Are My Sunshine' or 'Smoke Gets in Your Eyes'. There was a long menu:

Año del Guerrillero Heróico

Cóctel de langostinos, shrimp cocktail
Consommé Tapioca, tapioca soup
Lomo a la parrilla, grilled pork loin
Ensalada de berro, watercress salad
Helados, ice cream

One day there was no more butter, only lemons.

One evening there was a knock at the door from a man who was also living in the hotel and only talked in vague hints. He looked up at the ceiling and made signs, suspecting that there were microphones everywhere. For all that, he had nothing much to say. He complained about poor-quality razor blades, explaining in passing that that was just his paranoia.

———

You could have left the island as soon as it became clear no one needed you.

But now we really wanted to stay. I wanted to know what was going on behind the facade. We started to make contacts—the harbour district, the underground, genuine and false artists, dignitaries who'd been chucked out—we didn't care what their views were.

The other people who'd been washed up in the Nacional were also a good source. Every one had a story to tell: the man from Texas who'd hijacked a plane, the niece of a toppled president, or Roque Dalton, a poet and guerrillero from El Salvador who'd fled his comrades because they were after his blood. There was a German as well, a podgy man who didn't want to go into the Bundeswehr and had requested political asylum from the Cuban ambassador in Vienna, a diplomat of the old school. I have a soft spot for deserters, especially when, like this M., they know a lot about literature. Now he was sitting in his hotel room and had nothing to do. So he started to translate poems by Heberto Padilla. He introduced us to the poet with whom we became friends.

Now and then our minders would come and pick us up. They never told us they'd be coming, they just arrived. A surprise. They always enjoyed a joke, but they refused to tell us where we were going.

We get in. They chat to us a bit: Don't worry, everything will sort itself out. To put it in a nutshell— we're their guests, therefore they can do whatever they like with us. They drive us to the city centre where there's a crowd waiting. It turns out that they're taking us to the ballet. Pas de trois, valse noble, frenetic applause, it's one of the best companies in the world. Why do we feel relieved? Why are we confused when, late at night, the porter opens the car door and we go back into this modular stone building with its turrets and fortress walls? That's Stalinist architecture *avant la lettre*, for in 1930 the Seven Sisters of the Soviet model didn't yet adorn the Moscow skyline. The gangsters' castle is open—like a trap. But I'm not K. and as for the revolution, it's not taking place in here.

———

But you obviously liked the city?

Havana is decadent in the worst sense of the word, crumbling, rotten, worm-eaten. The old town with its *solares* resembles an anthill. The maze of passage-ways and bolt-holes with rats scurrying out of them recalls the Spanish quarters in Naples. In the court-yards there are sad palm trees and beside them shacks with lavatories and laundry tables shared by a hun-dred families. In decaying palaces a Caribbean version of the Soviet kommunalka is springing into life. The stairs are steep and dirty, the plaster falling off, the shops and bars are empty.

The capital is much too big for this country, and it has a big problem with the water supply since Havana hasn't got a river. In most districts, the taps run dry for three to six hours a day.

Underdevelopment, a rural exodus, overpopula-tion have drained the wealth from the metropolis. Even the richest areas have not escaped this trend. Once cabarets, country clubs, striptease joints and nightclubs were evidence of the dominance of the USA's entertainment industry, but the revolutionary government closed them down or put them to a dif-ferent use. The Yacht Club now houses the Workers' Welfare, the army has taken over a golf course, where they drill their recruits. But the main road from Miramar is still called Fifth Avenue, and the legendary Tropicana, that first opened in 1939, still brings in welcome hard currency, even if the 'paradise under the stars' puts on a more respectable front than in its more uninhibited days. This attraction is in the borough of Marianao and has a ballroom in which a thousand people can dance.

Varadero is an hour and a half's drive to the east. The place was once the preferred summer holiday resort of the affluent middle classes. It lies amid pine trees on a long, sandy spit. There are delightful old villas with their paint peeling off. The large verandas on wooden pillars recall the way things looked on the Baltic coast in 1910 or 1920.

Later on, the Americans came and built the first international hotel, a luxurious limbo. In the restaurant little pink table lamps illuminate the icy darkness to the wail of a mediocre big band. Now it's meritorious sugar workers and mechanics who sit there holding hands with their girls. There are many coloured people among them. They're only allowed to spend the night there on their honeymoon.

Far out and high above the dunes is the house of the Du Ponts, an imitation Spanish castle. Inside there are wooden pillars, balustrades of black oak and a loggia with Moorish wall tiles. Even the television in the unused library is in a medieval chest. There are plastic flowers on the Blüthner grand. The house organ, made by the American Aeol Pipe Company, is automatic; the cupboard has rolls on which medleys of the nineteenth century are stored. On shelves there are yellowing photos: the kindly master of the house playing with his dogs. His wife, a hysterical beauty, could have escaped from a novel by Scott Fitzgerald.

Just to remind you: Irénée du Pont founded one of the biggest chemical companies in the world. The firm is noted for products such as polyester, nylon and teflon. It also played a role in the Second World War, in the construction and running of the plant that produced plutonium. Little signs ask visitors not to touch the exhibits. Thus the revolution protects its cultural heritage.

The curators' treatment of another attraction, Hemingway's legacy, is equally meticulous. The major writer had more taste than the Du Ponts but less drive. His house in Havana, his park, his gardeners, his shoes and his books, his rifles and fishing rods indicate that, like the chemical industrialist, he had a tendency to accumulation, only he was interested in acquiring other things than shares: every lion's skin a *peau de chagrin*, every big-game trophy, a prelude to his suicide.

So you were having a holiday on the island?

They kept putting us off. There was no 'organ' to take on the two unemployed foreigners. Not that there was any lack of organizations in Cuba! Quite the contrary. When you arrive at the airport you're immediately asked, *Que es Su organismo?* Which institution is responsible for you? There is a work of reference that the ignorant can consult to find that out. Havana, unlike Moscow, does have a telephone directory. The first part, a substantial section on blue paper, contains an endless list of shortened names, a jungle of abbreviations from MINSAP to ICAIC, from ANAP to OFICODA, that makes it clear to everyone that all areas of social life are covered. Anyone who doesn't have a ready answer to the question of their *organismo* is given to understand that they're a kind of astral body that has no business there; anyone who cannot claim the patronage of an abbreviation is not regarded as a responsible adult.

Very plausible the way you describe the shortcomings of bureaucracy. But what about you? Correct me if I'm wrong, but do you yourself have a dysfunctional relationship with institutions, whatever their nature? You've never stuck it out for long in such organizations.

So what? In our case, we weren't put in the care of the scrofulous Writers' Association, which has never achieved the power and wealth of its Soviet model, but of the superior Casa de las Américas at Calle G in Vedado. They looked after foreign authors, including many exiles who'd been driven out of or fled their countries in Latin America.

The founder and director of the Casa was Haydée Santamaria. She was looked on as a heroine, not to say a saint, of the revolution because as early as 1953 she'd taken part in the crazy attack on Moncada Barracks in Santiago that ended in disaster. She was captured and subjected to very sophisticated torture: Baptista's men castrated and killed her brother, Abel, before her very eyes. But she remained silent and didn't betray any of her comrades.

She had, there is no other way of putting it, given of her blood for the revolution. Even years later, people were still talking about it. Blood and death are favourite terms in political rhetoric in Cuba. ¡Patria o muerte! That slogan has to be included in every speech of Castro's. But it was also quoted at many receptions, while the petits fours were being handed around. I found that somewhat macabre. Because of her heroic deed, Haydée could take some liberties, for example, as editor of a stylistically advanced quarterly that was to represent the best of Cuban cultural policy. The energy of the 45-year-old had survived all the ups-and-downs of politics better than her beauty. She wasn't an intellectual; overall, she cut a less arrogant figure than most comandantes.

I only observed one touching weakness in her. In her house everything looked expensive, the way some Parisian women like it—everything painted white, with a few personal photos and souvenirs. Her private bathroom, where I once ended up by mistake, housed an arsenal of the finest French perfumes. It never occurred to anyone to reproach her for this. Puritanism is against Cuban nature.

Was this woman you saw as a heroine not rather just a poor soul? She can't have pulled much weight. And I suspect you only saw Castro himself at his public appearances. Speeches lasting for hours, to an exuberant crowd on Revolution Square?

Not just that. At the beginning of our time in Cuba, when we were still in favour, we were invited to a peculiar state occasion that took place in a covered stadium. When we drove up in the car, guards with their rifles at the ready came up to the door. They announced our arrival by walkie-talkie and took us into an air-conditioned office with leather chairs and a glass-fronted bookcase against one wall. Two deputy ministers, the rector of the University and a dozen men in olive-green battledress were already waiting there. Coffee was handed around. Then the selected guests were allowed to take their seats on the empty platform in the stadium.

Whispers of expectation. Suddenly the playing field is filled with men in red jerseys. The two ministers are among them. And, towering above them is a heavily built, bearded man. It's the boss. They're all hopping about and weaving, sending hoarse cries and a leather basketball to each other. They shimmy up and down until the whistle goes. The opposition is a student team from the provinces. Even though the students seem to be well trained, after two 12-minute sessions the score is 104–72 for the government team.

During half-time the boss grants an audience to a few of the spectators, perhaps a Bulgarian trade delegation or a bull-breeding specialist from Canada. He is casual, relaxed, avoiding anything that might resemble a ceremonial state reception. It's an exotic show: a ritual contest, tribal culture, the king as centre-forward, after the victory comes the palaver. There's also a bandit-style element: Fidel as chief of a robber band, the members of the gang as courtiers. Robin Hood playing basketball. He wins, but always for the poor and dispossessed, of course. The guns are just shown at the entrance for security.

But I can also remember a mammoth rally on Revolution Square. On such occasions Castro always caresses the many microphones set up in front of him as he informs the people about his comprehensive knowledge of pesticides, of psychiatry or the advantages of atomic energy. There can be only one expert on the island, namely, him.

On that afternoon, however, he appeared as a specialist in genetics and dairy farming. The best cows of all, he said, were the F-1, a breed that would soon be supplying the infants of the country with milk. So far the revolution hadn't solved that minor problem. As usual, the speech went on for several hours.

A few days later I received a surprising invitation: the *Comandante* invited me to his private model farm. A few specimens of the above-mentioned milk providers were standing there, in an air-conditioned, clinically clean cowshed. He'd had them flown in from Europe, purchased the best milking machines and centrifuges and engaged a team of competent Swiss specialists: dairy experts, zoological geneticists and veterinary surgeons. An extremely ambitious project!

A few days later two men in uniform rang at the door of our room and handed me a package containing the proof of the quality of the cows: a carefully packed, round Camembert that, unfortunately, at a temperature of 35 degrees was hardly edible 24 hours later. The production of that delicacy must have cost as much as a new tractor. He also got a French sympathizer, the agronomist, René Dumont, who had advised him, to try it, asking him whether the cheese wasn't the equal of that from Normandy? Dumont couldn't bring himself to agree with that. The consequence was the immediate banishment of the agricultural expert.

However, the undeserved favour that had been granted us went round Havana in no time and brought unexpected benefits overnight—not just the previously unobtainable bulb for our bedside light but even an apartment.

———

Living in a hotel wasn't good enough for you then?

We moved into Tenth Street in Miramar. The house number, however, escapes my poor memory that is less bothered about forgetting than it ought to be. But what does that matter? It was Masha who managed to get us this apartment where the rich used to live, in the most comfortable part of Havana. With its stucco facade and palm trees it evoked Miami a little.

Unlike me, Masha had understood the rules that operated on the island from the very first moment. She felt at ease. She laughed at the illusions of visitors from the West who saw in Castro and his *comandantes* a last chance for socialism. But with me she showed astonishing patience. She was a good teacher because she thought that she did have to help me but there was no point in going on at me; with time I'd understand myself the way things were.

Of course, she immediately understood what the arrival of Soviet advisers at the airport meant. A horde of comrades from the Committee for State Security, known under the abbreviation of KGB, were ready to give their Cuban colleagues fraternal assistance. They came in civilian clothes, but they were easily recognizable in their shapeless suits.

Since 1960, Castro had had a countrywide surveillance system, the so-called Committees for the Defence of the Revolution. These little apartment-block supervisors were good for the odd denunciation but they were no substitute for a system of experienced specialists. The *Comandante en jefe* had never hesitated to get rid of his comrades-in-arms from the early years of his regime as soon as he found them a nuisance and he had enough prisons and internment camps to teach anyone who contradicted him a lesson. If necessary there was an execution squad ready for action. In the long run, however, such ad hoc decisions were inadequate to meet the demands made by socialism on an island. Sooner or later improvisation would have to give way to a system and that was what he lacked.

Even an experienced Russian such as Masha couldn't know that. She assumed that in socialism there had to be an all-powerful party and that to learn from the Soviet Union meant either victory or collapse.

I, on the other hand, gradually came to understand that there was nothing of all that in Cuba. A politburo only existed on paper; the Central Committee never met; and the cast-iron party discipline Lenin had drummed into the Russians didn't exist in Cuba. The place of Soviet power was taken by one single person, who was called Fidel Alejandro Castro Ruz.

———

For all that, I don't have the impression that your time in Cuba made the two of you depressed.

Far from it. We'd never got on so well together. Masha was happy. For the first time we managed to live together with all the everyday chores that involves—doing the shopping, cooking, sharing, grappling with details and purchases . . . As supposed 'foreign experts', special shops were open to us which had many things that were unobtainable for ordinary people in Cuba: rum, cigars, all sorts of foodstuffs, condensed milk, coffee—even toothpaste, bulbs and batteries. To my simple left-wing mind such privileges were suspect and I hesitated to exploit them. Masha thought my scruples were absurd. On the contrary, she said, we were positively obliged to make use of them. She immediately bribed Toni, the driver who had driven us around the country, to take us in his ancient Chevrolet to the shop for foreigners where we filled the boot with all the good things that were available.

From then on there were parties for all our friends in Calle 10. The playwright Virgilio Piñero, whom the Writers' Association had pushed out into the cold, was there and the writer and ethnologist Miguel Barnet, who was allowed to travel abroad as often as he wanted. Above all, however, we were able to supply the corpulent grand old man of Cuban literature, José Lezama, whose most important work, the novel *Paradiso*, had finally been printed, with Montecristo and Partagas, the cigars he'd had to go without for so long.

Other people, who weren't shadowy members of the literary world, were also welcome to Masha, who was an excellent hostess. They all sensed that she was the only Russian who had come to Cuba without a commission or instructions from the KGB. The men flocked around her and she loved that. Occasionally someone would bring a dubious acquaintance from the harbour quarter, where there were a few members of the demi-monde left. In such a society anyone can lose their job overnight because they shoot their mouth off once too often or because they're homosexual. I suspect that the odd elegant spy also turned up, but it never occurred to us to bother about that.

A favourite guest was Heberto Padilla, a man of about the same age as me and of a surprisingly sunny, open disposition, who could easily switch to and fro between seriousness and cynicism—a truly Cuban phenomenon. His tousled hair and large spectacles were an adornment to every one of our parties. He knew Russia and got on well with Masha. He dismissed his colleagues' concerns with a laugh, as if nothing serious could happen to him. We often went out around the town with him and his wife Belkis. His poems, that took no account of the standard rules of language, were circulated clandestinely among the free spirits. I liked some of these poems so well that I translated them:

My Travelling Companion

She throws her course book away
Marxismleninism
my travelling companion
She stands up in the compartment
and puts her head out of the window
and starts to shout:
Out there she shouts is history
out there something's slipping past
blacker than a crow
followed by a stench
stately as a king's arse.

Heberto came from Pinar del Río and was an inveterate smoker. He knew the USA really well; he'd worked as a correspondent in Moscow and that had made him immune to many illusions. In October 1968, a prize committee, to which Lezama Lima belonged, had awarded him the poetry prize for his volume of verse *Fuera del juego* (*Sent off the Field*). The Writers' Association had no choice but to publish the book, though the officials disliked it so much that they attached a page-long assessment warning against his 'counter-revolutionary views'. From then on, he was regarded as a deviationist, a mark of Cain that boded ill for his future.

But if I know you, you went about things pretty cautiously.

As far as possible, yes. You have to visualize it: at half past five in the morning there's a knock at the door of our room. Someone's asking for me. I wake with a start. A messenger boy gives me a letter, a package and a glass of tea. Everyone's in a bad mood because the coffee's run out.

The neatly wrapped package contains an old pair of tennis shoes. I get some trousers out of the wardrobe, pull on a shirt and read the letter: 'My dear friend, I popped around at four in the morning to bring you these wonderful shoes. They look as if they're a hundred years old. I hope you'll find them useful in the field. I can't come with you—yesterday morning I had a heated argument with the Director of my institute and absolutely have to sleep.'

I drink my tea, close the door behind me and rub the sleep out of my eyes. A girl in rags and tatters is waiting for me outside between two Cadillacs. We walk to the bus stop. Each of us puts five centavos in the payment box. The journey lasts three-quarters of an hour. We get off in one of the suburbs. It's still pitch dark, the streets are deserted. We make our way through rubbish, banana plants and goats tethered to a water tower. We ask an old peasant who's squatting there, 'Where are the writers?' His only answer is a vague wave of the hand. After some wandering around we come across a handful of yawning men, each one leaning on a hoe or a pickaxe. It's light now and we all go out onto the uncultivated land.

It's to be made into a plantation. The *Máximo líder* has decided in spring 1968 that 40 million little coffee trees are to be planted all around the capital. All 'producers of culture' have been called on to do voluntary work on Sundays—an idea that hardly seems original to anyone who knows the Soviet Union.

Who summoned you there? Did anyone force you?

No.

So it was your own fault?

Yes.

Go on then.

Then we all start to get the weeds and thistles out and dig little channels. Hundreds of little green saplings are brought from a truck. The plastic cover is removed, the seedling placed in the ground and the hole filled in. There are sham peasants working in other fields as well: in front the National Bank is hacking away, to our right the theatre, and right at the back the State Publishing House. Only the film industry seems to be playing truant. By midday the sun's burning like hell, we've got blisters on our hands. A man with a moustache appears on a skinny horse and, without a word, distributes bread. After two o'clock our tools are thrown into a pile and I set off home.

I meet the peasant again at the water tower. He's eaten his snack and is in a better mood than in the morning. Over a cigarette he tells me that coffee will never ever grow in that soil. The saplings die because it's too clayey and too dry. Everyone knows that. But no one asks us! In countries where a refusal to listen to reason has become the official attitude of the state, that's quite normal.

I stand in the crowded bus and watch the crumbling plaster, the pillars and balustrades of the slum housing in Vibora pass by. On faded inn signs from earlier times, you can read: 'The Four Points of the Compass', 'The Other World', 'Paradise, Steak 50c'.

———

Was that your only stint out in the fields?

Of course not! But in order for you to see my achievements in the correct light, I have to go back a little.

Feel free!

Do you know what an *ingenio* is? That's what the sugar mills have been called in Cuba since time immemorial; it's a word that's derived from the 'ingenious' monuments of the early industrial age. They were the 'satanic mills' in Blake's poem. In such places you can still find the old *barracones*, where the slaves used to live, and the steam locomotives groaning the way they do in engravings from the turn of the century. In machinery of huge proportions, human beings look small as they move on stairs, galleries and bridges. Huge flywheels, soot, immense cauldrons. Everything is steaming, thumping, hissing, grinding and rattling. Half-naked men are working in a tangle of pipes, conveyor belts and chutes. An old-fashioned labyrinth that keeps on having to be shut down for a few days, because the pumps are quietly rusting away and the old valves have broken down again.

———

Touching, this interest in sugar mills, livestock and produc-tion statistics in Cuba. It seems to me that in Germany swedes and cement factories tended to leave you cold.

Kafka wrote about the *Investigations of a Dog.* My ambition was more modest, but Cuba is a small coun-try and I thought it would be very suitable for some field work, even if the results left something to be desired. I don't know anything about dogs. But you can't dispute my fondness for the Cubans.

Apart from Castro—you weren't particularly fond of him.

He himself was responsible for the comparison with Don Quixote that you hear quite often. 'The revolution,' he said in 1966, 'has shown that in Cuba there are more Don Quixotes than Sancho Panzas.' Cervantes' novel was one of the first books he had printed, and that in an edition of 150,000 copies. Everyone was to read it. The statue that he had erected in the garden of the Writers' Association is further evidence that he identified with the hero. It portrays Don Quixote as an anti-imperialist warrior.

As is well known, his big mouth was the cause of many successes and many embarrassments. 'In 10 years Cuba will have the highest standard of living in the world,' he promised in June 1959; 'What use are words if the people don't enjoy the fruits,' he said in 1963; 'At the end of this year no items of food will be rationed any longer,' he declared in January 1965. No collection of his speeches has ever been printed. None will be allowed while he's still alive. History has to be constantly touched up and rewritten, a procedure that Castro took over from his Soviet models.

You have to give the *Comandante* one thing, though. He had no intention of submitting unconditionally to his Moscow ally. He had nothing against the deliveries of Russian oil, but he disliked the revisionist tendencies of Stalin's successors. It had already come to a really serious conflict in 1962 on the occasion of the so-called Cuba Crisis. Castro would have preferred to risk an atomic war rather than abandon the stationing of nuclear rockets on his territory. That dear wish led to his greatest humiliation. When Khrushchev and Kennedy came to a compromise over his head, he suffered one of his feared outbursts of rage.

Like most politicians, the omniscient *Comandante* was an ignoramus as far as economics was concerned.

It annoyed him that the economy refused to dance to his tune. Equally out of his depth was the unfortunate Ernesto Guevara who, as minister for economic affairs, had to deal with the problem of how to make toothpaste. As head of the National Bank he had to look after a currency that was hardly worth the paper on which it was printed.

They were always organizing new campaigns, announcing new plans to put an end to the chronic shortages. The secret of how the regime managed to let even the tropical abundance of fruit and vegetables vanish without trace, will presumably die with him.

———

One day Castro suddenly remembered sugar. Ever since the days of Spanish and North American rule, sugar farming had been both the basis of the island's wealth and its curse. Eighty per cent of its exports came from sugar. Even as far back as the end of the nineteenth century José Martí, the prophet of the country, had declared, 'A country that bases its economy on a single product is committing suicide.'

Initially the revolution intended to put an end to this monoculture. Production was lowered. Between 1960 and 1969, with falling prices in the world market, between 6.7 and 3.8 million tons alone were harvested. 'About turn!' the *Comandante en jefe* cried in October 1969. Undaunted, he announced, 'Next year Cuba will be the biggest sugar producer in the world.'

At a blow, production was to rise to 10 million, the ultimate *zafra*. Overnight on the Rampa, Havana's show street, where there were neon adverts but nothing to buy, a Warhol-type display appeared, noisy and flickering, with crazy neon arrows and stars, promoting the sugar harvest.

This project led to perhaps the greatest economic fiasco the Omniscient One brought down on his country. In 1969 and 1970, economic activity in Cuba came almost to a standstill. Universities and schools, factories and offices were closed for months on end. Everyone had to volunteer for the *zafra*, the sugar harvest. Whole divisions of the army marched off. They were not only to go and work in the fields but also to see that military discipline reigned.

The minister with responsibility for the sugar industry explained to the *Comandante en jefe* that the target was unrealizable. He showed him that the physical capacity of all the sugar mills was insufficient to process such quantities. The old machines, he said, could only be kept operating at 40 to 60 per cent capacity because they constantly needed repairing and because there were no spare parts. As well as that, there were no locomotives only ox-carts for transport. The boss was annoyed and asked the assembled comrades, 'Which revolutionary has the courage to replace this ditherer and take over the task?' Immediately a few who were immune to facts, raised their hands and the failure was dismissed on the spot. He knew what he was talking about and events proved him right.

Where did you get all that from? Were you there?

The dismissed sugar minister told me himself. The *zafra* was a failure, of course. Even though Castro's attempt to break the record paralysed the whole country, all they managed was a meagre eight million tons. The sugar industry rapidly went downhill and it has never recovered from the excessive demands made on its resources.

––––––––

But you didn't let yourself be put off, you went out into the fields, your machete in hand.

That wasn't for that harvest but a year earlier, during the miserable *zafra* of 1969. I certainly didn't want to join a brigade of revolution tourists, blond Swedish women, hippies from the Middle West, young ladies from the Auvergne and rebellious seminarists from El Salvador who wandered around the sugar fields of Camargüey carrying large knives. They had themselves filmed and liked to give interviews. Some were soon too tired to think about what the point of all their enthusiasm was.

No, I preferred to be with the ordinary Cubans who had been sent with their machetes to work on the harvest. After work in the improvised tents with their three-story bunk beds you could find out how things really were in the 'first liberated territory of North and South America'.

Would you like to hear a few lines of poetry?

You've even written a poem about it?

Yes. It's called 'A Camp in Toledo'.

> The clatter of the dominoes on the kitchen
> table,
> the rustling on the bunk below me:
> the distinguished man from the Congo is
> reading an old number
> of *Le Monde diplomatique.*
>
> The bush knife being honed on a file,
> the cough and whimper of the radio.
> Between two Brazilian hits
> under the corrugated-iron roof Dubček
> resigns.
>
> Through the window is our countless foe,
> that is supposed to save the country,
> remorselessly rampant and tall and juicy:
> the green canes; black against the sky
> the column of smoke motionless over the
> sugar mill.

Your repertoire seems to be endless. But it might also be the case that no one wants to hear about this ancient history any more.

Then let's just stop.

Now you feel insulted. Should I leave?

You can stick your fingers in your ears. As a foreigner you're often approached by children in the parks of Havana, and also in the village squares in the provinces. Three girls, two black and one white, ask me politely for some Shicklet. At first I don't understand what that is. Then it occurs to me that they probably mean the American brand of chewing gum.

'How do you know what that is?'

'From the old days.'

She means: from the time before 1959.

'But I'm not American and I don't have any Chiclets for you.'

'Then you must be Russian.'

'No. I come from Germany.'

'Is Germany as beautiful as Cuba.'

'I like it there, but I like it here, too.'

'You have everything over there in Europe.'

'Yes, if you've got money. But why do you have to have Chiclets?'

'We want freedom *and* Chiclets. I suppose you don't like chewing gum?'

'Not particularly.'

'That's because you in Europe have everything. People always want things they don't have.'

All that word-for-word, uninhibitedly, seriously, as if it had only just occurred to them there in the park.

————

That's all you have to tell us?

No. Do you know what a *posada* is? There have always been hotels in Cuba that let rooms by the hour for lovers. Before 1969, Havana was the biggest brothel in North and South America. Only the New Left in Europe thought the posadas were a revolutionary invention for sexual liberation. All that was new about them was that now these establishments were run by the state or, to be more precise, by the Empresa Consolidada de Centros Turísticos. Not all of them were said to be as filthy as La Diana on the Malécon. From what I heard, there are mattresses there full of diabolical springs and the towels aren't clean.

There's a large selection of posadas. The clientele can have a look at others, for example the Musical, the Canada Dry, the Chic or the Encanto. Authorities on the subject know that there is one, that isn't in the telephone directory, where you can drive up in your car; that's El Monumental.

Men queue up outside these places, especially at the weekend. They have to register; they aren't asked for their ID card. The woman remains unseen, waiting around the corner or in the courtyard, until the man has been given a room. Then she's let in through a back door.

The first three hours cost 2 pesos and 60 cents, three with air-conditioning, though I was told that the machines generally don't work. A room waiter will bring beer or rum. In some establishments the desired drink is hoisted up in a basket. The walls are so thin that every transaction about change can easily be followed.

The Pullman has a large wall covered with political posters, two red flags and a portrait of Che Guevara. At the bottom it says—at least, so it is claimed—*El mejor servicio al pueblo*! A certificate attests that the employees there have fulfilled the targets in the Plan with revolutionary consciousness. A notice in the rooms says, 'Since the start of the revolutionary offensive we no longer accept tips.'

That's good.

What is remarkable, given all that, is the show of puritanism the regime feels obliged to put on—the official segregation in schools and harvest camps, and the hypocrisy of the Minister for Education, who says, 'As long as appearances are kept up, they can do as they like as far as I care.' Abortion is available free to everyone; no questions are asked. The pill isn't available because it is supposedly too expensive but pessaries are automatically prescribed by doctors on demand.

The worst aspect of their revolutionary sex education, however, was the witch-hunt against homosexuals. Special forced-labour camps were set up for them, the notorious UMAPs (Military Units to Aid Production), to which the 'work-shy, counter-revolutionaries and the immoral' were sent to live under concentration-camp conditions. Men who preferred men were meant.

This of course involved the Cubans in a futile struggle against themselves, for on this subtropical island sexuality has taboos but no limits. Even in the heart of the capital, at night male devotees of forbidden love sometimes used to meet in the Cemeterio de Colón, the biggest graveyard, right beside the flower-strewn grave of the miracle-working Milagrosa, beneath the gigantic plaster angel protecting her—a sign that, whether sooner or, as is to be feared, later, any doctrine is doomed to failure given the contradictions and anarchy of the people here.

One of the reasons for this might be that in Cuba there is often room for magic and education inside the same head. I once met a female official who represented the Women's Association and a trade union. This old witch of a black woman was an adherent of Santería, a widespread Afro-American cult from the days of slavery. Scholars like to call that kind of thing a 'popular' religion. They say that many of the rites come from West Africa or the Congo. Drums, dancing and intoxicating music are certainly part of it. In a trance a Catholic saint is transformed into an African divinity. Thus, in Santería, the red-haired Saint Barbara, patron saint of the artillery, becomes Changó, the warlike Orisha of thunder, a belligerent god of the Yoruba.

But that's far from being the only result of Cuban syncretism. The old fighter for the Women's Association told me that she's not only possessed by the gods and saints of the cult but also by Marxism. As a matter of course she knows about fortune telling and the healing powers of certain plants. She doesn't read books but loves a juicy story. She can have her say in discussions on culture and education, she says, for she attended a seminar not long ago and since then she knows about 'ideology'.

Some *comandantes* are also adherents of Santería and in their private capacity take part in the rituals whilst others prefer spiritualist seances. Everywhere the evil eye is feared. Once, as a joke, I told the culture minister, 'Anyone who is against me dies. I don't know where it comes from, I never invoke it. Unfortunately that's just the way it is and I can't do anything about it.' The minister touched wood. Two months later he was dismissed and banished to a distant province, where he promptly died of a stroke.

———

You're particularly fond of that kind of anecdote. Do you seriously believe they say anything about the revolution?

I know that historians refuse to take stories like that seriously. But that's a mistake. They often tell us more than any theory does and they have the advantage of being short. Would you like to hear another?

Get on with it then.

One evening the telephone rang in our room. A woman I didn't know was on the line, asking if we could arrange to meet. But why did she want to meet me? 'Because of my admiration for you.' A few further questions show that the caller doesn't really know whom it is she admires, or for what reason. It looks like a clear offer. In all socialist countries you can meet young women like that in the area around international hotels; whom they're working for is another question. The unknown woman is persistent, she tries three or four times.

By chance I made her acquaintance some time later at a party. S. is pale and thin but with traces of former elegance. Once obviously pretty, perhaps beautiful, she now looks ravaged. Alcohol or drugs? Her hair is dyed red, her eyes heavily made up. Looks like 40 but is probably considerably less.

She's the daughter of extremely rich parents, landowners from Oriente province. At 17, after a crash course in first aid, she went into the Sierra.

That was in 1957. She had a love affair with Camilo Cienfuegos, one of the heroes of the guerrilla war whose death, after he had been demoted by Castro, remains a mystery. Even today S. has a huge photo of this revolutionary hanging up in her room. At the time her father was pro-Castro; like many rich Cubans he wanted to get rid of Batista, but didn't take Castro's rhetoric seriously. From the guerrilla warfare in the mountains his daughter knows almost everyone who counts in Cuba today. ('Back then I bandaged up all these heroes. They whimpered like little babies.')

After the victory of the revolution, she worked for the state security service. After a few months came the first conflict—she refused to spy on her comrades from the Sierra. Arrested, four months in prison without being sentenced in court; her connections helped her to get out. She married a young doctor who divorced her when she refused to emigrate with him to the USA, where he lives and prospers today. Then she fell in love with a Spaniard who had an import–export business in Havana and worked in his office. One day Fidel Castro appeared there and recognized her. 'You here? Why are you helping a capitalist? Why aren't you working for us. Here, give me a call.' She still has the piece of paper with the secret number in her handbag and shows it to me: 'There! The proof.' She claims she never rang him. Why not?

The Spanish businessman left Cuba in 1966, his firm was taken over by the state. She has a Spanish entry visa in her passport, but once again refuses to leave the island. The Spaniard still sends her remarkable letters.

She gave up work. Her father is still in the country spending the compensation for his property that was expropriated. She cables him and gets him to send her 2,000 pesos. Her apartment is big enough for her to invite friends whom she feeds, pampers and puts up for days. That's why her huge refrigerator, a 1958 model, is usually empty. Then she buys what she needs on the black market. She moans about everything and seems apathetic but still, especially when she's drunk, claims to be a revolutionary. 'Socialism, what a stupid word, those soap-box orators make me sick, but what do you all know about the poor Cubans? The cause is necessary, it's inevitable, moreover, it's a Cuban cause. Foreigners should keep their traps shut.'

But she only sleeps with visitors from abroad. 'Cubans treat their women poorly and are unfaithful to them. But when their wife is unfaithful, they go mad. When they're satisfied they sleep like logs. They don't talk to you at all.' She changes men as often as she changes her clothes, but she's extremely jealous. When there's a nude scene in the cinema she'll ask her friend, 'Do you fancy her?' and get furious if he doesn't say no.

She makes her clothes herself. She makes nothing out of the foreigners. She's convinced she's kept under surveillance. The neighbourhood committee with the apartment-block supervisors regard her unfavourably. Her father would like her to go back to live with him but she tells him she doesn't feel like living out in the provinces, and nothing would make her work in agriculture. After that he didn't send her any money for a month. He'll just have to accept that she won't allow herself to be blackmailed.

I met her at Cookie's. Cookie earns her living by playing at being an attendant in a Turkish bath in the old town. In that run-down establishment, jazz musicians, would-be poets and photographers meet for melancholy soirées. Poems are improvised or someone puts on a scratched Beatles' record. Beer and rum, 25 or 30 pesos a bottle, is brought from the black market. A few mulattos go there too, with their Swedish girlfriends who are worried about interior design in Cuba; they complain about the government's poor taste. Fidel—a shrug of the shoulders. A French woman explains why planning will never work. A homosexual complains about the repression. The usual jokes are told once more ('Fidel dies and goes to heaven . . .'—'Fidel talks to his dead mother . . .'). Some are unemployed, others hold on tight to their fictitious positions. They're not interested in the revolution but they don't want to go to

Miami either. Where does the money they spend come from? The mood is one of despairing exuberance. After 20 minutes the record is changed. All that doesn't bother Cookie, but S. seems to be at the end of her tether.

———

You're telling me all this to divert attention away from yourself and from what was happening in Berlin.

In April 1968 the bars there were teeming with activists though no one was entirely sure whether they were active in the party, in student politics, in street fighting, or in bed.

On Maundy Thursday some poor soul, incited by the gutter press, shot Rudi Dutschke three times in the head with a pistol, injuring him so badly that his life was in danger. On the same evening a few thousand people went to the Springer building in Kochstrasse and tried in vain to storm it. With the encouragement of the usual agitators a few cars were set on fire. That was the beginning of the so-called Easter unrest—blockades, demonstrations and street battles in 20 towns in which at least two people died.

Once again I wasn't there; instead I was sitting in a living room in the Prague suburb of Vinohrady, in the apartment of my friend and translator Josef Hiršal. His wife Bohumila served us some *Liwanzen,* yeasty pancakes with plum jam. I don't think we talked about the Prague spring; we argued about the future of experimental poetry.

On 1 May I was back home again. The media in Berlin were fuming with rage—the May unrest in Paris, student protests in Poland and Gomulka's campaign against 'Zionism', the escalation of the Vietnam War—the whole world seemed to be on fire. And yet the mood during the great May rally in Neukölln after the shooting of Rudi Dutschke was strangely subdued. I wasn't the only one who had the feeling we were on a sinking ship. Naturally no one would admit to that.

But soon there were more and more signs that the high point of the revolt had passed. On 30 May, with the votes of the grand coalition, the federal parliament passed the emergency laws. In June, de Gaulle was returned to power. The May events in Paris were over and in August the Soviet invasion put an end to 'socialism with a human face'.

———

Where were you all that time?

I can't remember.

So, black film—blackout. Should I give you a clue? Does the name Lehning mean anything to you?

Oh yes, now I remember. I was in Amsterdam a few times.

Pleasure trips, I assume. Or did the Dutch welcome you with open arms?

Well, they had translated some of my stuff even though the *Moffen*, as the Germans are called in Holland, are not exactly welcome there. In those days they quite often slashed the tyres of tourists who longed for a pipe of hashish. I told my publishers I was exactly like the others but they refused to accept that. I didn't like the much-admired display windows in the Walletjes where the whores wait for their johns. I went off to see Arthur Lehning.

He was a man of many addresses. If you were lucky, you could find him on an island outside the mouth of the Scheldt, in an attic in Ménilmontant, in a back room full of conspirators somewhere in Barcelona, a farmhouse in the Massif Central and even in far-off Djakarta for a few years. Isaiah Berlin saw to it that he was elected a fellow of All Souls in Oxford, one of those shabby-genteel secular monasteries that you only find in England. It is evidence of the self-assurance of a civilization when it is capable of co-opting an old anarcho-syndicalist and as well as his opponent at London University's Birkbeck College, the stubborn communist Eric Hobsbawm.

Best of all, though, was to meet Arthur Lehning in his old quarters on the Amstel. The brightly polished brass signs on the doors never had degrees and titles, as they do at the homes of respectable people, who at 25 had already given up trying to find out who they were. Mostly the telephone rang in vain and in the Institute they'd just say. 'Arthur's out.'

He was one of those who, years ago, founded the Instituut voor Sociale Geschiedenis (The International Institute of Social History) on the Herengracht in Amsterdam. Its archives have survived crises, revolutions, moves, a world war and an occupation, and anyone who has never worked there can have no idea of the treasures it holds.

I know little about Arthur's heroic days. I got to know him as a 70-year-old gentleman with shaggy hair receding at the temples, not the young man with a sharp profile, full of fighting spirit, who in the 1920s published the only four-language periodical in the world. It was called *i10*. A few lines aren't enough to list all the contributors: Schwitters, Benjamin, El Lissitzky, Arp, Gropius, Kandinsky . . . and so on.

Naturally Arthur has remained and anarchist *sui generis*. Not a cartoon anarchist carrying a bomb with a lighted fuse, the way the fears of the bourgeois like to portray them. The *weledelzeergeleerde heer*, the very learned gentleman, was a nomad, a bird of passage, who didn't leave behind a nest but a pyramid of knowledge. The *Archives Bakounine* has grown into a life's work. Every few years Arthur presents another of those large, blue-black volumes in four or five languages. I only hope he never flies away from us for

good, from us, the younger generation with the
clumsy gait.

––––––––

But I hadn't finished with Cuba.

No one's interested in the sordid details any more.

I wanted to say something about the human-being
factory.

If you have to.

The building in Calle Carlos III, a busy traffic artery,
used to be the flesh-market. The big building is
guarded by policewomen carrying rifles. It's open
inside, you can see into the separate floors like
arcades. A rectangular concrete ramp leads up from
the courtyard so that you can get up to the attic floor
without having to take a single set of stairs. Gigantic
posters on the walls announce, 'Cuba will triumph!
Cuba—an example to the whole of America!'

First of all, the human being is designed, based
on half-tone photo engravings and oleographs from
old encyclopaedias. A powerfully built black man
carefully copies a plaster skull and paints it. Others
are making plaster legs, plaster breasts, plaster hands.
A few yards further on, in the next room, these
models are cast. Then comes the actual production
process. Four hundred former civil servants are
working in a large hall.

The person is made from old newspapers that have been soaked and are then pressed into a hollow plaster mould and dried out. Once a day the mould is opened and the human being is born. It's full of holes, fully grown, rough and empty. Brain and lungs, heart and spleen, bowels and sex organs are all missing. It's open, hollow, unprepossessing; leading articles from the Party newspaper can be read on its skin. Then it's scraped smooth and polished. At the next table a woman dips it in garish green paint: that's the primer. Next an eerie pink is slapped on. An old mulatto puts on the muscles with an ox-blood-red brush. At other tables, in other troughs, the brains are made—dozens of yellowish spheres, all cut in half, with bluish veins. Sullen bureaucrats paint on tonsils, gall bladders, wombs. A neatly dressed, bespectacled man is working on a half cut-open breast. A fat woman is dealing with the legs, her speciality is a particular bone. The legs are hanging horizontally in a frame, slowly rotating. Even when the person has been finally assembled, it is still rotating on its axis in a long narrow box with one bearing at its head, the other at its feet; a few yellowish sinews are added. Finally the human being is given a little black number. It can be taken to pieces at any time. The colours are crude, monstrous, diabolical, and they appear to have been devised for that purpose alone, for you don't find them anywhere else in the world.

Not everything produced in the factory goes with this human being. For example, there's a long row of enormous ears, on a scale that would be more appropriate to an elephant. Strange formations behind the external ear seem like geological formations. They also produce the embryos of calves, rennet stomachs, rectums and fleshy structures of which it is unclear whether they are meant to represent the intestinal villus or sick oranges with greenish eczema.

All these objects are made by hand, bit by bit. The human-being factory is an abattoir in reverse, backwards vivisection. The old smell of meat, penetrating, ineradicable, still clings to the walls, the stone tables, the cobbles of the courtyard.

The factory is shown to visitors with pride and satisfaction. The output is around three to four hundred persons per year. That is the target in the plan. Everything for education!

Before the revolution only a few private schools in the capital had teaching aids. For a while the government brought in expensive teaching materials from East Germany. A minister who disapproved of this expense went through his staff, found dispensable people, discovered a meat market where there wasn't any meat any longer, looked for plaster, paint, waste paper, found some, took a couple of specialists into custody and created this monument of unintentional surrealism. Everyone who's working away with a paintbrush shares his relaxed attitude, his confidence.

Can you tell me what this factory is? A socialist grand guignol? Or a papier mâché torture chamber?

To me it seemed like a malicious parody of the socialist concept of the New Man. Moreover, it shows that it's easier to transform underdevelopment into art than to abolish it.

———

All of that has nothing to do with you. You remind me of Rumpelstiltskin in the fairy tale: 'Oh how glad I am that no one knows my name is . . .' Can we please get back to Masha and you.

Even if the stories of other people are more interesting than our own? For example, the one of the unfortunate Italian who came to a sad end. He was originally from Piedmont, where his father had a farm. He didn't want to stay there. He went to Turin and became a metalworker. He was a member of the Communist Party for 15 years. He was fairly seriously injured during a demonstration outside the American embassy, not by the police, however, but by the Party's stewards. He was carrying a picture of Che Guevara and slogans calling for an armed struggle. He'd got the idea from a series of articles in *L'Unità* in which guerrilla warfare was presented as the only way to establish socialism. The author was also taken to task, though without a thrashing. The journalist went to Havana as a Party liaison officer and newspaper correspondent.

When he was 34, P. gave up his job. He'd managed to save enough to travel to Cuba. There he tried to make contact with the emissaries of Latin American guerrilla groups. Asked what had given him that idea, he named his countryman, the journalist. When the Cuban authorities asked the latter about P. he told them that he could give no guarantee for him, P. could just as well be a CIA agent. It didn't occur to the security service to seek information on him from Italy.

By this time P. had volunteered to work in agriculture. Soon he had risen to *trabajador de vanguardia*. His keenness didn't make him any more popular with the other farm labourers. Impatiently he waited for news from the capital, but people there seemed to have forgotten about him. Months later he returned to Havana off his own bat and did the rounds of the various offices. Each of them passed him on to the next because none was responsible for him. Finally he went to see the Italian correspondent in his apartment. He told him he could do nothing for him and, anyway, guerrilla warfare on the continent was over and done with.

On the same evening P. went to a little party. The guests were mostly foreign, exiles from Nicaragua, Venezuela, and Colombia, plus a plane hijacker from the USA and a few Cuban officials. P. praised the food, drank a little then announced to everyone who was willing to listen that he was going to commit suicide in the course of the night. At around five in the morning he slashed his wrists in his room. He lost consciousness but didn't die. He woke around eleven and threw himself out of the window.

Neither the journalist nor the Italian embassy did anything about P.'s funeral. Foreigners who had got to know him at the party, asked after him and learnt that for weeks his body had been in a freezer compartment. They paid for the hearse that cost 15 pesos. A so-called pauper's grave was found for him in the graveyard. The dead man had not wanted to have a cross on his grave at any price, but at the *Cementerio de Habana* crosses (at 1 peso and 40 centavos) were obligatory. A small group of mourners took the cross; the strongest of them, an engineer of athletic build, bent it as much as he could before it was set up.

P.'s widowed mother in Italy, not having heard from her son for months, wrote to every possible official body in Cuba, but her letters remained unanswered. Finally she came across a small advert in a communist evening paper. A woman worker from the Cuban province of Matanzas was looking for a pen friend in Italy. P.'s mother responded with a long letter in which she asked the recipient to pursue enquiries in Havana. The Cuban woman had the greatest difficulty with the old peasant woman's Italian. She couldn't decipher her handwriting or her spelling, had no idea what it was about and passed the letter on to the Ministry of the Interior. That set off an investigation. The people who had given P. lodging were suspected of murder. Even the comrades who had arranged his funeral were arrested, interrogated, etc., etc. . . .

————

What's that meant to prove? That it wasn't just all fun and games in Havana?

That would be nothing new. In the summer of 1968, there was a flourishing black market. One pound of rice in the shop: 18 centavos, on the black market: 3 pesos; 1 ounce of coffee: 0.95–5.00; a filet steak: 1.00–25.00; a pair of nylon stockings: 2.00–12.00. I was offered 30 pesos for my Polaroid glasses. Workers sold shoes they'd made from old car upholstery and strips of leather they'd stolen from their shoe factory. Imported machines were taken apart while they were still in the harbour and cannibalized for spare parts that were lacking everywhere.

These activities were stimulated by a 'revolutionary offensive' that the government announced in the summer of 1968—the closure of the lottery, the bars and pubs, the expropriation of the small traders, hairdressers', laundries, workshops and private restaurants. The queue outside the nationalized pizzeria grew ever-longer. Professional queuers appeared on the scene who, for a cigarette or a piece of sugar, would get a *turno*, that is a place in the queue for the following day. People were forbidden to receive parcels from relatives abroad. The tobacco rations were drastically reduced. And that all under the slogan: THE FIGHT AGAINST SELFISHNESS.

The effect was devastating. The Cubans, who lived in one of the most fertile countries in the world, had too little to eat. There was no fruit and hardly any meat. What the people found perhaps even harder to bear was having to give up non-essential things— cigars, coffee, rum. Since criticism wasn't allowed and open resistance impossible, the people fought back with the black market, looking after one's own, with theft and bribery. A new vicious circle had begun— the less there was to eat, the more police there were and the less the police had to eat, the more corrupt they were.

In our country the explanation for that is always underdevelopment. Only no one seems to know what that is. I believe that what is meant by that is more a way of living than a precise concept. The economic mechanism can be grasped most clearly, for it obviously has its roots in colonization. What is more difficult is to distinguish the variants in mental attitude that have resulted from it—the interplay of different traditions in the way people see themselves, the way they see power, compromise and corruption.

This mixture is particularly evident in Havana. Not just because wealth and poverty are adjacent in the same street. Symptoms such as the generally prevalent machismo are connected with it. Balls are constantly mentioned—it's important to have *cojones*. Castro sees himself as a model of this. It's clear that this is where the rejection and persecution of homosexuals comes from. And the particular form of racism you encounter in the Caribbean derives from its colonial history. There is a richer vocabulary for the gradations of skin colour than elsewhere. Thus it is that a mulatto feels far superior to a black, even if no one will admit it. No one connects that with the anti-imperialist rhetoric which, as everyone knows, denies what everyone knows. The same is true of the repeatedly proclaimed abolition of prostitution. An aspect of underdevelopment, in the wider sense, is also the everyday deal by which loyalty is exchanged for pay and obedience for toleration.

———

You're beginning to bore me with your Cuban stories.

As you like. I was also in Stockholm a few times during that year.

I'm not interested in that.

You're not? Have you forgotten her?

Who?

Nelly. Nelly Sachs.

How dare you! I was her friend.

Exactly. Stockholm was closer to my house in Norway than Rome or Prague, so I kept turning up in her tiny apartment on Bergsundsstrand. She was almost 70 then, and had left the media response to the Nobel Prize behind her. Even in the middle of the tumult you entered a different world in that place of refuge that belonged to the Jewish Community. Naturally I knew something about her life and could sense the burden she bore. I was careful not to torment her with the usual questions. No interpretations, no attempts to 'categorize' her poetic *oeuvre*. Even admiration can be tiresome when the admirers keep pestering you.

While Nelly Sachs prepared supper in her little kitchen—she was a very good cook, by the way—we first of all talked about quite ordinary things: our families, her doctors and ailments or one or other of the Swedish poets she was translating. She seemed happy that I avoided any high-flown emotionalism and never mentioned the fact that she was a seer, perhaps the last in a venerable Jewish tradition.

In fact I fear that many of her admirers misunderstand mystics. They think of them as saints, shut off from the world, as if Hildegard von Bingen had never recommended a herb for impotence, or Jakob Böhme never picked up a cobbler's awl, Swedenborg never made a name for himself with inventions for mining. And as far as the Hasidim are concerned, they have a real sense of humour. Quite a particular sense of humour, true, light as a feather and not one that everybody can understand.

Many people from the enlightened Stockholm bourgeoisie or those she knew from the literary world have helped her. But there were also others who were close to her. There was a woman who lived next door whom I will never forget. She was called Rosi Wosk, came from Hungary and was a survivor of the Auschwitz death camp. She was always there for Nelly, not just when she was in a bad way, when she felt sad or needed some particular medicine. Often she'd only run out of milk or salt, or a pair of shoes for her tiny feet needed to be bought, or a light bulb changed. This woman, who had been severely traumatized, radiated a great sense of strength. She, taller and far younger, had taken over the role of mother and looked after the poet. She was the only one in the building who had a TV and sometimes Nelly would knock at her door. Then the two of them would secretly watch a film or a football match.

That all sounds pretty credible.

I've got other things that will amuse you. I can tell you where Moscow shone or what happened in Berlin-Moabit.

Was that before or after? You're mixing everything up.

Do I have to keep on drumming into you what a tumult is? If you're looking for a bookkeeper of our past, you've got the wrong man. If that gets on your nerves then we can give up this conversation as far as I'm concerned.

No, my little lad, you just keep on going.

I'm not your little lad. I was 38 when all that stuff started, much too old for the so-called student movement, the APO and all that. Universities were never my territory. I had no business there. I thought I should leave it to the professors, lecturers and students to haggle over their staffing pyramids, tripartite parities and intermediate examinations.

What I did like, however, was the disruption of the traditional social order in Germany. That was long overdue and difficult to stop. *Antiauthoritarian*—that was the catchword. It didn't bother me that I myself was in danger of becoming a kind of authority, even if against my wishes and only a mini-authority.

All that's probably of no interest to you. But then I've no time for your serene detachment.

Nor I for these things you get worked up about.

What do you mean by that?

I mean all the jargon and the clamour of the revolution.

That Red thing was the very worst the Federal Republic could imagine. And not just the government, but the people as well. Most of those who went on about revolution just used the word to frighten the ordinary citizen and they succeeded in that. I never really believed them.

OK, then let's watch the next sequence of your film. What do you see now?

Paris. I'm asking myself why it's so quiet on Place de Clichy. The city seems to be completely deserted, as if a state of siege had been declared. The streets are gleaming in the rain. Suddenly sirens can be heard. A bomb detonates on Piazza Fontana in Milan. Elsewhere the crunch of tank tracks. An old factory with mattresses spread out all over the floor—probably in Berlin-Moabit. People clad in exotic rags are staring at three black-and-white TV screens that are running concurrently, but with the sound switched off. On one of them there is psychedelic twitching, on another an advert for a detergent, on the third people on fire can be seen. From the loudspeakers comes the booming sound of 'All You Need Is Love'.

Please, that's enough of your tirade.

It's not something I've made up, that's the way it was.
A confusion of noises, planes landing, shots in living
rooms, slogans, shrieks, memory gaps. A station on
the Moscow Metro. There's an argument. A drunk
and an army veteran are having a fight. The armed
police are called. The same as ever. In a Berlin car park
a young man who's been shot, his face can't be made
out. A cluster of freezing demonstrators outside the
Prussian Supreme Court—the building's been empty
since 1948. Until then it was the headquarters of
the Allied Control Council, the highest power in
Germany after the war. The usual barbed wire, the
usual water cannons, the usual arrests. On the rest of
the spool there's just a jiggle of scratches.

Or I see before me the judge delivering summary
verdicts in the New York Night Court. A resigned,
stocky, white-haired, sympathetic man, who has
to pass sentence on the drug-dealers, rapists, bag-
snatchers who appear before him thick and fast. Don't
worry, he's leniency itself, mostly there's a small fine
or a few weeks of community service, shovelling
snow or sweeping the streets. Only at the third
offence does he finally put the accused behind bars.

And what's the self-employed day trader, a former
Peace Corps worker, doing in his pad on MacDonald
Street? He's sitting at his calculating machine. There's
a large bag in the bathroom full of white powder that

has a funny taste. When dawn starts to break, he needs another dose. He has to stay awake because the Tokyo stock exchange is open while Wall Street is still asleep.

Robert Rauschenberg put a little aeroplane on the roof of his house in SoHo and painted it in a patchwork of colours. That district of Manhattan is teeming with galleries and artists who daub the walls with protests and portraits of secular saints. No subway carriage without graffiti. The sprayers who spray silhouettes of Che Guevara on fences around building sites and garage walls have rationalized their work by using templates.

The rest of that roll of film is just black.

Now do you understand that the tumult can't be neatly trained on a trellis?

————

Are you saying that sometimes when you woke up you'd no idea where you were?

Yes, that's exactly what happened. It was as if the silence was packed in cotton wool and there was a smell of snow. That must be birchwood, I thought. Who can have lit the fire while I was asleep? Was it the Russian Nyanya?

In other places there were other smells. Of disinfectant? Of gas? Of vomit? The blue water in the swimming pool tasted of chlorine. The pipeline was broken, the Caspian stank of bitumen and sulphur.

Another time there was eucalyptus, hibiscus, Bougainvillea and that sexual scent of moss and deer in a borrowed bed that was more overpowering than the tropical flowers on the veranda . . .

———

A flight without end. But not as in Joseph Roth's novel where it's a matter of life and death. The whole thing is just a tragicomedy.

The comedy was unintentional. I once had to spend two days waiting in Karachi. Lifeless people were lying on the pavements. Some still breathing. It smelt of decay, of shit, there were bluebottles everywhere. The flight reflex was stronger than sympathy and curiosity. I got myself to a safe haven, one of those Sheraton hotels that had always repelled me with the sterile uniformity of their bathrooms, where the outside world drips off you. And that was where I barricaded myself off from the wretchedness, in the same way as I sometimes leant back in a Lufthansa plane that was taking me, exhausted by far too many brief glances at primeval forests or deserts, back to Frankfurt.

———

Or to Moscow. You were going to tell me that the city shone, even if only in particular places. I wouldn't have thought that possible.

Do you know the Kutuzovsky Prospect? It's one of those magnificent but inhospitable avenues in which Stalinism took such pride and that nowadays look sorely in need of repair. The building at number 12 conforms to this legacy with its dark staircases and a lift that's usually out of order. The retired generals and senior civil servants who live there look like ghosts themselves.

Behind these walls a two-room apartment with kitchen conceals a sublime secret, the sole elegant literary salon in the capital—and probably in the whole country. This place doesn't owe its lustre to the drawings by Chagall and paintings by Pirosmanashvili on the walls, nor to the illustrious visitors from all over the world—the prima ballerina of the Bolshoi, film people from Italy, writers from Latin America and couturiers from Paris, but to the woman who receives them. Her name is Lilya Brik.

When I visited her for the first time, all I knew was that she was the widow of two famous men with whom she had formed a passionate *ménage à trois*: Mayakovsky and Osip Brik. Only later did I learn that Lilya's widowhood was far more extensive. One of her husbands is said to have been a Red Army general who fell victim to the purges of 1937. Now she's married again, to a man who has made a name for himself as a writer of film scripts. He helps the maid as she serves drinks and canapés, and positions himself modestly behind Lilya's chair.

When I met her she looked just the way Viktor Shklovsky once described her: 'She had chestnut eyes, was pretty, with red hair, slightly built. Her acquaintances even included bankers and other fossils. She loves drop earrings in the form of golden flies and old Russian bejewelled crosses, possesses a string of pearls and is festooned with all sorts of junk. She could be melancholy, feminine, conceited, fickle, proud, amorous, clever and all that at the same time.' It may not be gallant to mention her age, but even at over 70 she still manages to flirt.

She is completely Russian and a complete cosmopolitan. Her literary verdicts are feared. She seems to be familiar with everything. Everyone who goes to see her is asked, 'What's new in your part of the world? Why do your politicians look just as ugly as ours? What's the avant-garde doing? What are people wearing this winter?' She regards socialism as a mistake, capitalism as stupid. She helps Russian poets as long as they're young. Patiently she removes one set of blinkers after another from them. They love going to see her, for Lilya loves them and the food is good, perhaps the best in the whole of Moscow. As soon as her young poets become stars, she loses interest in them. 'The poor things,' she says. 'They've already been taken in by their success.'

She knows how to intimidate bureaucrats, which is more difficult in Moscow than elsewhere. She ignores the microphones that have doubtless been inserted into the telephone. She talks with breath-taking openness about Stalin, about the 1930s and 40s, and about betrayal. She names names, everyone comes in for it at some time or other and only very few escape unscathed.

Once a year she goes to Paris to see her sister, Elsa Triolet, and her brother-in-law, the famous parlour communist Louis Aragon. Yves Saint-Laurent idolizes her and promises to design costumes for her. I think she sometimes gets tired, but she doesn't let it show. She would think it impolite to be bored.

She has many enemies in Moscow. She's too sharp-tongued for her fellow countrymen, too beau-tiful, too witty and too independent. What they most take amiss is her greatest merit—she can't stand memorials. With skill and endurance she's opposed the many attempts by the bigwigs to turn Mayakovsky into an official plaster saint. She's charming, she's unbribable. In the eyes of the society she lives in, those are two unpardonable faults. Moscow's not a particularly amusing city. Without Lilya Brik it would look even greyer there.

————

By the way, I met Neruda again in Moscow. Whenever he went to Russia the best room on the best corner of the best storey of the Hotel Nacional, within easy reach of the Kremlin, was made available for him. He immediately invited me to breakfast. The waitress in her cap and white apron brought the trolley with everything he asked for: caviar, blinis, champagne. Ideological questions he waved away. 'What are you doing?' he asked. 'When are you coming to Chile? What do you want to drink? Coffee? Tea? Vodka? Here, a present for you, my latest book, a luxury edition, there's only a 100 copies.' Then he inscribed a dedication in his sweeping scrawl. Naturally I wasn't the only one to be treated in this manner, for he liked to hold court in his hotel suite. He saw it as a matter of course that he was entitled to all this because he was a poet. Neruda managed to ignore the fact that that myth was dead. He behaved as if he were Lord Byron, though his famous predecessor presumably paid his own bills. This flamboyant posture had become second nature to him.

Further evidence of that is the museum he's had built on Isla Negra in Chile. He was an unscrupulous collector of art and trophies. I once saw how, when invited by some Russians of discriminating taste, he knelt down before a picture he liked. He couldn't take his eyes of it, he told his hostess, who was so astounded she ended up giving him the object of his desire. It was difficult to take offence at his enthusiasm. He was a master of survival but calculation was far from him. He had no need of it. Sometimes he was a child, sometimes a grand seigneur, but always a poet.

———

And what about you? Who found accommodation for you? Who paid for you? Wasn't it this or that foundation? Writers' Associations? Goethe Institutes? Arts Councils? Estate owners? Wealthy universities?

You know very well what happens when a scribbler makes it to the invisible xeroxed list that all those who have a bit of money to spare, and their committees, photocopy from each other. It's like the accumulation of offices in politics.

It wasn't meant as a reproach. We both know there's no such thing as clean money. No state that prints it can control it, and no minister of finance knows where it goes. The fact that it goes through so many hands is the nice thing about cash. And that's why you have to wash them every evening. Tell me about your prizes.

Most of them I forgot as soon as the money had gone. Once there was a bit of a stir. That was in Nuremberg. They gave me 6,000 marks and I passed them on to a few old communists who had been sent to prison because they didn't accept the ban on the German Communist Party. It is said that at that time the public prosecutors in Germany looked into ten thousand possible political offences, because people were convinced the enemy was on the left.

The money was no more than a drop in the ocean, of course. The city council and the press got themselves worked up about it. That's enough about that.

I have to admit that in the middle of the tumult I also accepted a prize in Sicily. Don't ask me when, or how many lire the cheque was for. There was a reading in Catania, in the magnificent Teatro Massimo Bellini, and a luxurious hotel in Taormina. But that was nothing compared with the appearance of Anna Akhmatova on the same stage a few years earlier. I still haven't forgotten her performance. The way she, at 75, sat there like a queen on her throne, a proud beauty whose poems had, after decades of torment, triumphed over her opponent, Stalin. Once she'd learnt them all by heart then burnt them: 'Hands, matches, an ash-tray, a ritual beautiful and bitter.' That's the way Lydia Chukovskaya described it to me in Peredelkino.

So with their antiquated pomp the Italians got it right for once. Two years later, the unapproachable queen of Russian poetry, who never abdicated, died in Domodedovo . . .

But to get back to Cuba . . .

That's an idée fixe *of yours.*

In that case, we'll just have to talk about something else.

You hung around Rome as well.

That's where I made friends with Carlos Franqui. He was a Cuban writer who was one of Castro's companions in the very early years. Together with Guillermo Cabrera Infante, the most malicious and clear-sighted polemicist in the country, he founded a weekly called *Lunes de Revolution* (Monday of the Revolution). It was silenced as early as 1961 and Cabrera was shunted off to Brussels as cultural attaché. A few years later he resigned and went into exile in London.

Cuba again!

Yes. Carlos Franqui stood it longer there. I knew his voice because he was one of the questioners in my 1974 play *Havana Inquiry*, and I knew that for decades he had resisted in vain the gagging of the free spirits who remained. He was well acquainted with the inner workings of the regime. He refused to accept its approval of the Soviet invasion that put an end to the Prague Spring. He preferred exile and poverty in a room in Rome to an open break with Castro. It is he and our mutual Sephardic friend, Laura Gonsálvez, whom I have to thank for helping me avoid doing some stupid things in the middle of that chaos.

I was there so often that I'm probably getting everything mixed up again. When I was in Trastevere I always used to go and see Laura, who worked as a badly paid editor for Einaudi. She knew more than I did. On the one hand, she was highly trained in languages and on the other, she knew the Italian Communist Party and everything that was happening in the Italian left-wing inside out. She could speak Spanish, had been to Cuba, kept me up to date about Carlos Franqui's experiences and more than once put my naivety on the right track.

It have the feeling that back then I was also with the beautiful Kiki and the proud Massimo in a bar on the Via Veneto, not far from the American embassy where the stones were flying. The tear gas drifted over to where we were. Then we went dancing, with Ingeborg Bachmann, who was wearing a gleaming, sequinned dress, arm in arm with Ungaretti.

I've just about had enough of your name dropping!

Oh, we were all famous back then. We were just as happy to sit at a table with obscure journalists as with Carlo Emilio Gadda, Cesare Cases and the stingy Alberto Moravia, even if *la dolce vita* was long since past and gone.

Not a word about Hans Werner Henze? That's odd. You knew each other, were both extremely taken with Havana and worked together for a long time. That was something! An opera, all sorts of music . . .

He lived in a sumptuous apartment in an old building in Rome, next door to Sandro Pertini, the president of the Italian parliament. On his grand piano he had set up signed photographs of musicians, theatre managers and singers. At the front were those with whom he was on good terms, rivals and opponents fell into disfavour and shifted towards the back or were simply removed.

At that time I was still in his good books. I enjoyed working with him in Cuba just as much as in Marino, where Hans Werner had acquired the manor house of La Lepara in the Alban Hills. Is it a fact that the estate once belonged to the Colonna family that used it as a game preserve? All I can say for sure is that the composer looked after Rudi Dutschke and took in refugees from the German underground, although what he liked best was to sit in his soundproofed study and compose.

He used to write letters to me in his jittery handwriting on blue rice paper. But one day, I've no idea why, our friendship was gone and we never heard from each other again.

———

You've always remained true to your Scandinavian predilections?

Yes. I was often in Sweden. I had hardly any problems with the language there, I could read everything and get by reasonably well with my Norwegian.

We've done Stockholm already. I presume you took a break from the tumult in the social-democratic neutrality there.

Oh, there were troublemakers even there. A little group of students, four lads and three girls from the well-off middle class, had somehow managed to end up in the labyrinth of left-wing sects. They wanted to put an end to their illness—the bourgeoisie and put their ideology into action. They barricaded themselves in their apartment on Östermalm, stocked the fridge and exercised self-criticism. Each of them had to sit on a chair in turn and account for their background, their life and their views. As it turned out, there was no New Man (or Woman) among them, therefore the seven decided to intensify the interrogation. Anyone who gave wrong answers or lacked the requisite militancy, was hit and beaten up, with their permission, of course. After a week there was hardly anything left to eat and they only had the odd hour's sleep. Then one of the girls ran off. She escaped through the bathroom window and across a balcony.

Apparently she still gives the impression of being disturbed. Now she's working in a factory on the edge the town and incites the workers to take action. But she literally speaks with a forked tongue—in her normal alto voice when she's talking about the class struggle but when she describes her nightmares to the doctor she changes to a falsetto, a monotonous whistling singsong. She refuses treatment and when she runs into one of her old comrades in the town centre, she crosses to the other side of the road.

The other six ended up in an ecstatic state somewhere between euphoria and despair. On the twelfth day one of the lads had a serious political relapse. He expressed doubts about the revolution and the ability of people to be changed. The group then decided to take him to court. They condemned him to death. The lad accepted their sentence; he realized, he said, that he was a hopeless case. It was beyond his powers to attain a new consciousness. They tied him up with curtain cord. It was ten in the evening in the early summer. The nailed-up door was broken open. One of them fetched the parked car and they carried the deviant, unnoticed by anyone, out of the lift, loaded him in the car and drove to the harbour. Since they had no guns and were trying to avoid leaving traces, they had decided unanimously, including their condemned comrade's vote, on death by drowning. They parked the car at the quay, failing to see a no-waiting sign. A police car happened to be passing, stopped, demanded to see their papers and finally discovered the trussed-up man in the back seat.

The encounter with the police—it could just as well have been a postman or a cleaning woman—was like opening a safety valve. It was their first encounter with the outside world, with reality, for 10 days and it had the effect of an explosive shock. Instead of running off or resisting, the six of them, including the condemned man, burst into hysterical laughter. The police, assuming they were drunk, gave them a breath test, sniffed around in vain for drugs and finally let them go.

They separated, without mentioning the Great Chairman. They'd nothing more to say to each other. When matter and antimatter meet, they disappear in a sudden discharge, leaving nothing behind. Isn't that what it says in a myth invented by contemporary physics?

I don't believe a word of that. Where did you get it from?

From someone who knows that milieu very well. From a reliable source.

Second-hand information, that is. Hearsay. Just a rumour, political gossip. Or you're simply lying.

———

I've no need to do that. The facts are improbable enough. You only need to listen to what happened next to M. You remember, the student who'd refused to go into the army and fled to Cuba because otherwise he'd have ended up in jail. He was totally incapable of fitting in. They'd given him a job teaching German, just to get him off their backs, but he lost it because of his womanizing. On top of that, he defended the homosexuals whom Castro had sent to labour camps. After five minutes of 'voluntary' help with the harvest he was quoting Adorno. He never left the comfortable hotel, where he'd been given accommodation as an asylum seeker, without a supply of handwritten notes with his telephone number that he would distribute to mulatto women he fancied, both out in the streets and on the bus. He boasted that he'd had great success with this method.

It was in this way that he found his Evangelina to whom every few days would take pots and parcels of provisions from room service to Guanabacoa, a township outside Havana where there was hardly anything left to eat. That, he said, turned him into a rabid anticommunist. He wanted to divorce his wife, who'd stayed in Germany and was desperate to marry his Evangelina.

That sounds like a burlesque on your own love story.

Do I have to put up with your stupid remarks? He'd picked that woman up off the streets.

So what? And what was the end of his novel?

He was so desperate he begged everyone he knew, including me, for a few dollars. In the end, the Cubans expelled him as a 'politically unacceptable element'. Evangelina, with no money, passport or visa, had to stay where she was. Later I heard that the deserter had found another woman who possessed more cultural and financial capital.

————

I'd also like to tell you about the 'worms'. That's the official term for those who want to leave the country while it's still possible. That isn't just the rich, the dispossessed landowners, people in the professions and the functionaries of the abolished dictatorship, but also farmers, priests and small tradesmen whose businesses had been nationalized. They queue outside the foreign ministry, the Spanish and Swiss embassies. They're easily recognized from their isolation, their fear and their whole bearing.

They wait before the flights leaving for Madrid, pressed against the glass walls of the departure lounge hoping they might still get a seat while we, Masha and I, that is, already have our boarding cards.

Suddenly they appear as victims and we as virtual winners. They assume we're on the side of the guards in their olive-green battledress. That gives their silence a sense of appraisal. The feeling for friend and foe is exceptionally well developed in Cuba. On both sides we felt uncomfortable, uneasy.

Finally the plane took off. There were three old farmers on board. One of them came into the cabin holding his missal and breviary. 'I've got them here, my papers,' he said to the steward. 'You don't need them any more, *Señor*. You can put them away.' How long was it since they'd been addressed by that word? It was intoxicating! The women had put on their best clothes for the journey, the expensive velvet gown, the little embroidered handbag, hats and veils. Teenage girls scribbled excitedly in their autograph books. '*¡Ah la buona comida!*' the drunk, emaciated farmer cried when the meal was served.

In Madrid, at four degrees below zero, they were met by an ungainly Dominican monk. Hands clasping their throats, handkerchiefs pressed over their mouths, the emigrants stepped down onto foreign soil.

———

Once you told me about the heavy iron shutters over the doors and windows of the Old Town in Prague, about rusted locks and huge keys, dark churches, facades with the plaster falling off and the hotels for foreigners on Wenceslas Square. There were girls who could only be had for hard currency, secret police, conspiratorial whispers . . . Or was that earlier? When? 1964? 1967?

The pictures of Prague are difficult to date. I'd have to rummage through old postcards, gather newspaper cuttings, reconstruct biographies. I'd rather not bother with that. Only the iron shutters are still there, the bars of that irrepressible storyteller, Bohumil Hrabal, that drunks are already staggering out of in the morning, the corridors in which the Stalinist corpse is slowly rotting away, the stones in the Jewish graveyard, the rattling trams from the prewar years and from today. But exactly when that was, I can't say.

It was only later that the forbidden comments went out into the streets. Two thousand, twenty thousand, two hundred thousand words. Demonstrations, resolutions as well, power struggles, manifestos, rumours, basic demands, a fever of expectation. What did that furious movement have to do with the other furious movements, with the charades in Paris and Berlin, the precarious idyll of Peredelkino, the Bolivian guerilleros' wanderings right around the world, the firestorm on the Mekong River? Everything and nothing. How can I 'understand' all that at the same time, 'make head or tail of it', 'sum it all up'?

While there was seething, though non-violent, unrest on Wenceslas Square, I went up the stairs of an old building and entered the strange calm of a dimly lit room crammed full of everyday objects, books and pictures. That was where Jiří Kolář worked.

Two drawings that he gave me, and that you can hold in your hand if you doubt what I'm saying, prove I'm not imagining that scene. But was that large room with all its nooks and crannies, an attic? In the afternoon or the evening? I couldn't tell you the date or the address.

Jiří Kolář didn't talk much, just laconically showed you his works, the silent tumult of his materials. An untiring, inexhaustible omnivore whom nothing escaped, not a single scrap of paper, a remnant, an allusion, who took history as a whole, in all its greatness and baseness, and undid it year by year, sliced, cut, tore it into pieces and, without commentary, stuck it back together again in a different order.

The silence in his studio picked up the noise of the outside world like a radio telescope. 'The real achievement of the poet,' Osip Mandelstam says, 'lies in his noticing things.' The room was full, overflowing with a strange serenity. This Sisyphus didn't sweat. He had all the elegance and lightness of touch of an old master. He's turned 70. Not long afterwards he had to exchange his Prague studio for a little rented room in Paris. I know that it's crammed full with paper and pictures, with spoons and crutches, scissors and jugs, that in his hands speak to us just as they did in Prague. It's still calm where he lives. Jiří Kolář is alone. But he hasn't given up.

———

A few weeks later, Dubček took over the political leadership. I met two of my literary friends in a café in an arcade. One of them had been a communist until 1948. I listened to them talking about the events in Paris, the avant-garde, about Mao Tse-tung and the Vietnam war. It ended in a furious argument. One was so angry he got up and left without a word, and the other said to me, 'I don't give a shit about politics. I'll never concern myself with them again. For me art's the only thing that counts. Everything else is a con.'

A few hundred yards farther on, in the courtyard of Charles University, I met two students, who were wearing the little red Mao badge. 'In the past that wasn't possible,' they said. 'But now the CSSR's a free country.'

That wasn't the view of the bearded philosopher, a Cuban who lived in Moscow and liked to call himself a 'nonconformist'. He spoke disparagingly of the cult of personality in the West, where people held up portraits of Che Guevara and Mao Tse-tung at marches. It served the French students right, he said, that the police had beaten them up. It was a good thing for the whole world. It didn't bear thinking about what would have happened if they'd got the upper hand! Tear gas was much too soft a way of dealing with them.

I didn't feel like contradicting him or any of the others.

――――――

Poor T.'s fate was quite different.

I don't know who you're talking about. I don't like your abbreviations.

I'm not naming names.

How very considerate. But who knows what things you're going to make up now.

You don't have to believe me. But this T., another young writer, looked almost like a peasant, although he was said to have been a typical intellectual from Havana, multilingual, highly-strung and witty. In the spring of 1968 he was allowed to travel to Europe. He was particularly taken with Italy. He wanted to see Michelangelo's *David*. But the gallery was closed, supposedly because it was in need of repair. A friend told him that was just a pretext. In fact the administration was afraid of a group of Maoist students, who'd threatened to paint the statue red with a paint gun.

He travelled on to Venice. The city he'd dreamt of since he was a boy was a marvel for him. But the students told him that it would be necessary to tear it down after the revolution since the Venetians lived in intolerable conditions, making a living from exhibiting their own squalor to the tourists.

In Rome he told me that one of his Italian friends was propagating these ideas. The son of a wealthy family, he was one of the leaders of the student movement, a sensitive intellectual, of great aesthetic sensibility and the translator of T.'s own poems into Italian.

That wasn't an isolated case. It isn't that long ago that poor B. in Berlin received an unwanted visit from a so-called commission. Three comrades with deadly earnest expressions told her she was being considered as a candidate and began an interrogation. 'We must point out that Comrade H. will note down everything you say.' So recruiting a new member began with a police dossier. In that way a self-appointed avant-garde goes back to the worst traditions of Russian Party history—informing on others and blind obedience.

'The tradition of all dead generations weighs like a nightmare on the brains of the living. And just when they seem to be occupied with revolutionizing themselves and things, creating something that did not exist before, precisely in such epochs of revolutionary crisis, they anxiously conjure up the spirits of the past to their service, borrowing from them their name, rallying cry and costume in order to put on a new scene in world history in this borrowed language.'

You know your Marx.

I'm quoting him from memory. We must proceed in the same way as he did and ruthlessly dismantle all our predecessors.

––––––

But are you the right man for that?

I don't know.

When I went back to Prague, the spring dream was all over. The Soviets put an end to it with their invasion of August 1968. Did it have to be a Russian plane in which I flew to Ruzyně? But there wasn't any other route because we were on our way to Havana. Masha and I, a Russian and a German. Anyone hearing us talk was bound to see us as belonging to the occupiers. Almost exactly 29 years ago, the German army had marched in and only a few weeks back the Soviet tanks were rattling along Wenceslas Square. There was an apathetic calm in the streets. Only at the university were people still on strike. As a precaution we spoke in English, hoping that no one could tell where we came from by looking at us. The telephone network was still working so we rang friends because we knew that even in this terrible situation there'd be a welcome for us from Josef and Bohumila Hiršal in Vinohrady and Jiří Kolář.

––––––

And then the pair of you were back in your uncomfortable Havana.

There's one thing you can take from me—it's not only the abrupt changes between zoom and wide-angle shots that distort perception. The chaos restricts your field of vision as well. That's why I didn't hear much of the things other people were concerned with.

In July 1969, German newspapers reported on the following events, that they considered important. I quote:

> The General Council of Andorra has announced that they are extending the right to vote to women; however, the ladies will still not be allowed to take on government posts;

> A German singer called Alexandra has had an accident in Schleswig-Holstein—who does not know her 'Song of the Taiga'?

> A hundred thousand people were out to greet Pope Paul VI in Kampala;

> The Council of the Central Bank has raised the minimum reserve ratio by 10 per cent; and

> Meta Antenen from Liestal has raised the world record in the woman's pentathlon by 23 points to 5046.

I noticed no more of that than I did of the emergence of the Internet, that in those years crept out of the Arpanet—an idea of the Pentagon. I didn't miss the two Americans landing on the moon in the same month, even though I find space travel rather boring, but in general I suffered from tunnel vision that left out not only the *faits divers* but also many important things.

Why did we have such a fixation with Vietnam that all the other armed conflicts that were going on at the time concerned us far less? At least two million died in Nigeria because Biafra wanted to separate from the central power. There were dangerous skirmishes on the Amur; there was fighting in Guyana, South Yemen, Kenya and New Guinea; Northern Ireland, Columbia, Kashmir and the Basque country were close to civil war. One could still make jokes about Honduras and El Salvador, though there were two thousand dead in the so-called Football War. But even the Six-Day War between the Arabs and the Israelis was overshadowed by what was happening in Vietnam.

I've often wondered why that was. Very few Germans of my age have a tendency towards anti-Americanism. I can still remember the moment when I saw my first US soldiers. It was in a village in Franconia. There were five black GIs sitting round a fire, smoking. They'd come with a huge column of tanks and simply flattened everything to do with Hitler's regime. That was marvellous. I breathed a sigh of relief and chatted with them. They weren't in tatters like the German soldiers. Their uniforms were ironed and they brought goods that were unfamiliar to us. But what was more important was that they had something that didn't exist in Germany, something that began with D, E and M and was also known elsewhere, for example, in England, Switzerland and Scandinavia.

I wasn't the only one who liked that. And the disappointment at the US government when their soldiers held pistols to the heads of little yellow children on the other side of the world was all the greater.

———

It's your own fault if you first idealize a superpower and then get indignant when it doesn't correspond to the image of it you've made for yourself.

> We didn't know that the party had long been
> over
> and all the rest was a matter
> for the departmental heads of the World
> Bank
> and the comrades from state security. [. . .]
> That must have been in June, no,
> it was the beginning of April, just before
> Easter,
> we were going down the Rampa,
> it was after one, Maria Alexandrovna

looked at me with an angry glint in her eye.
  [. . .]
We were talking in a mishmash
of Spanish, Russian and German
about the terrible sugar harvest
of Ten Million Tons, today of course
no one talks about it any more. What's
the sugar got to do with me, I'm a tourist!
the deserter exclaimed, then he quoted
Horkheimer, Horkheimer of all people
in Havana! We also talked about Stalin
and Dante, I can't remember why,
what had Dante to do with sugar . . .
These foreigners who have photos of them-
    selves taken
on the sugar fields of Oriente, machete
    raised
high, hair matted, cotton shirt stiff
with syrup and sweat: superfluous people!
In the bowels of the capital the old misery
quietly continued to rot away, it stank
of old urine and old servitude [. . .]
And that thin man, going around
Havana, excited, absentminded, caught up
    in arguments,
metaphors, endless love affairs—was that
    really me?
I couldn't take an oath on it.

———

No one's bothered about your oaths. And what about Nelly
Sachs? You didn't concern yourself with her any more?

Oh yes I did. When I was in Stockholm again, she
complained about the men lying in wait for her outside the entrance to the building on Bergsundsstrand.
She could hear the voices of the men who were after
her exchanging messages about her whereabouts by
walkie-talkie on the other side of Lake Malar. And
they could eavesdrop on us when we were in the
kitchen. I knew from experience that any attempt to
persuade her that these fears were figments of the
imagination would be futile. 'Let's go to the back of
the flat,' I suggested, 'where no one can hear us. That's
out of the range of the agents' aerials.' On the balcony
I explained in a whisper that her pursuers had been
brought under control. All countermeasures against
them had long since been taken. I managed to calm
her down more than once but my ploy couldn't keep
her recurrent fear under control in the long term.

A few weeks later she had to give up her apartment. The doctors in Beckomberga Hospital, where
she spent the last years of her life, and her Swedish
friends did everything they could. The last time I went
to see her, she gave me a poem on blue paper. Her
handwriting was difficult to decipher. But right to the
end she had no doubts about her mission in life.

OK. But there's something else I'd like to ask you. What can you tell me about your involvement with the Red Army Faction? You did know Ulrike Meinhof, didn't you?

Of course I knew her. At that time she was living alone, somewhere on Unter den Eichen, separated from her husband, a left-wing speculator. She'd given her children up for adoption. She was a well-known and aggressive journalist. But that wasn't enough for her. Her foster mother had infected her with an essentially German form of Protestantism that she never shook off. She was lonely, a nun with no abbot. I felt sorry for her. When she took her glasses off, she looked defenceless.

Pacifism, social work, political agitation, none of those acts of penance satisfied her. Writing a column, wasn't that something for softies? When the first cars were set on fire all that merited was a brief report in the newspapers; the only point of such actions seemed to be to make the front page of the popular press. Ulrike Meinhof joined in the absurd discussion about violence that people were getting worked up over at the time. Violence against things or against people? To me such abstract ideas were like running on a gymnasium treadmill—they were absurd and didn't get you anywhere.

But then one afternoon in May 1970, four people, completely out of breath, appeared at my house in Friedenau: Ulrike, Gudrun Ensslin, Andreas Baader and a fourth I can't remember. They'd come straight from Dahlem where they'd forcibly liberated Baader, who was in gaol for arson, while he was out on day release. I realized they were on the run but I had no idea what they'd done. It was only later that I learnt that a librarian, whose name, Linke, ironically meant 'left', had been seriously injured.

They hadn't prepared a hideout and wanted to stay with me. I told them why that wasn't a good idea. For some time now there'd been a black Volkswagen parked outside my house with a man who had the tedious job of watching who visited me. I wasn't bothered by that. I'd even got into conversation with the envoy of the Political Police by asking him for a light. So I told my uninvited guests that the fuzz would certainly not be long in coming if they were to stay here. At that they quickly disappeared again.

My interpretation of this episode is that the RAF developed by accident. The only aim of their first armed action was to save an accomplice from spending two years in gaol. No thought of a political aspect or a strategy for future actions. By doing this they'd found themselves trapped in a situation with no way out. Going underground, they had no other choice but to seek safe houses, get money by robbing banks and invent ideological reasons for their actions. The outside world was irrelevant. They pursued their political careers at the cost of isolation and losing their grip on reality. It didn't need a court to condemn them to that.

Later, Ulrike Meinhof sent me a secret message from the underground by a roundabout route. Go-betweens guided me to a safe house in Hamburg where she had barricaded herself in with her fellow outlaws. She had summoned me in order to deliver the orders from their little group that now went under the grandiose name of Red Army Fraction. The pastor's daughter Gudrun Ensslin, who had turned into a guns and clothes fetishist, was also present. Undisputed leader of this phantom army was the abominable Andreas Baader, a crook on the run who had worked as a model for a gay magazine and loved most of all, apart from himself, fast cars. The women had submitted to him unconditionally. He treated them like a pimp. Ulrike despairingly went on about the necessity of bringing down the 'system' by violence. I told her that I had no truck with that sort of fantasy. Baader pronounced judgement. I was unanimously declared a coward because I had no desire to take part in their tests of courage. What I didn't tell them was that 30 years ago a 'troop leader' of the Hitler Youth had made very similar demands on me: I was to jump down from a high wall, just to prove to that supervisor that I wasn't a scaredy-cat. It didn't make sense to me.

I heard no more from poor Ulrike Meinhof, who eventually committed suicide. It was the courts and the Federal Criminal Investigation Department, the media and the authorities responsible for defending the constitution that finished her off.

———

Not long ago a woman friend of mine from Turkey brought an old letter you wrote to her during those years. Should I read it out to you?

I'd rather you didn't. I can imagine what it's like.

Don't worry. It's less embarrassing than lots of things you said back then. Listen.

This is the way things are here today, on the third Sunday in Advent, 1969: the Frankfurt Marxist-Leninists have split up into ML-1, ML-2 and ML-3. The money's swirling around in the streets, people are shouting in the stores, festooned with Christmas parcels. Great progress has been made in the liberation of mankind: pornography and Mao, all stuck up on the one wall. No one knows what's true and what's lies any more, everything's mixed up like a hashish vision. 'Turkish Red' is very popular here and the police are powerless, not as far as the future is concerned, but for the present because they have other things to worry about.

I often eat by myself unless I go to London to see Masha in Battersea. There you always have to have half crowns in your pocket, otherwise the gas runs out and it quickly gets very cold. It's 15 below zero during the night. I've got the flu. I'm not unhappy. In Cuba they battled with the sugar in vain and their shirts are still soaked in sweat and quite encrusted from the juice. I can remember, it's awful work. Everything's strictly rationed there. I'm a real oldie now but I'm still gadding about like a grasshopper. New books appear every day. I've almost stopped reading them. Actually I ought to be working but I often don't feel like it. I've got enough money. Olivetti have put an ad in the magazines with the picture of Che Guevara and underneath it: 'We'd have taken him on right away, we need people like that.' Another advert has photographs of 50 bottoms. Our society is an advertising hoarding on which something new appears every day.

I've come to the conclusion that we shouldn't allow ourselves to be killed. Mostly I even refuse to get annoyed. There's a stream of people going in and out. They want a flat, or to tell their stories, or to know what they ought to do, or money. I hardly ever chuck them out. What I like best is when they eat up everything in the fridge or go away with a pair of shoes. I just don't want to get annoyed, I'm too old for that now.

———————

But not too old to settle in Norway with your divorced wife again.

There's no question of that. At most I spent two weeks there. You know very well how pleasant that is. In three days the water in Tjøme makes your hair and your skin 10 years younger. You can wear a shirt for a whole week. The white and ox-blood-red houses: colours you only see in adverts now, in the great metropolises. The transparency of the north, a natural world that hasn't yet been devoured by history. That which stands aside doesn't grow old.

There are few excuses there, just the luxury of silence.

No telephone, no urgent work, no appointments and deadlines. I felt as if I were still 24 or 35. And as in my younger days, I would go to the letter-box in the hope of finding a message from the outside world. No one has tarred over the old paths by the beach. The bus driver still knew me. The next-door neighbour came over for a drop of Linie Aquavit. You remember the label with the guy sitting on a brandy barrel next to a sailing ship? 'Løiten Brænderi's Destillation Oslo' it says on it. The postmaster's wife said hello, the kiosk was still in the same place, the boccia balls were lying in the grass, just as they were 10 years ago.

There was only one thing that disturbed the quiet of the rocks, trees and the bay. Dagrun, the most gentle of women, had signed up with a Marxist-Leninist party. The simple world of the *Peking Review*, as if traced on carbon paper, seemed even more exotic in rural Norway than in Berlin. The need for religion can conquer all doubts. Stony-faced, that delicate creature explained to me that the Moscow trials were a model of popular justice, not to mention Trotsky— that traitor had received his just deserts. It was only bourgeois propaganda that defamed Comrade Stalin. The Russian communists who perished in the gulag were enemies of the people, revisionists, spies. True, some over-zealous functionaries had made the odd mistake, but Stalin had known nothing about them. In this version, the *diabolus ex machina* was called Khrushchev. It was with him that the death throes of the October Revolution had begun.

At times the naivety that expressed itself in such talk came close to madness. Dagrun's young comrades from the small town proudly bore the picture of a murderer on their way to liberation.

What did you say about that?

I waited until the torrent of words was over. But to the extent that 'bourgeois intellectuals' are really needed so that the sufferings of whole nations are not brazenly suppressed, I wish this category of people a long life and hope that it will even survive capitalism.

––––––––

Did you work a bit as well? You were going to write a whole book about Cuba, weren't you?

I tried to. I'd put together a pointless collection of material, any amount of statistics, quotations, price lists—a mere accumulation of facts for the sake of facts. That I abandoned the idea wasn't because of some remaining self-censorship, not wanting to kick a dog when it was down but, above all, because I found the whole thing boring. Thus my project just petered out.

In Havana I'd eventually started to feel like a left-over from a distant future, so I just made a little public gesture of farewell, an analysis I sent to press in 1969: 'Portrait of a Party'. A whole 25 pages for anyone who's still interested in that kind of thing. People in Havana were much displeased but there were no serious consequences for the author, as I'd left the country a few months earlier.

Once again you'd escaped unscathed.

Yes. But there were two things I wanted to do with that essay—to show Castro's admirers over here that I refused to be intimidated by them, and his official team that they shouldn't see me as a propagandist. The response was correspondingly furious both here and over there.

Six months later, Castro did me the favour of disavowing the most fanatical of his supporters.

———

How did it come about that both of you left your temporary island paradise for good?

You know from your own experience that there are grey areas in every dictatorship. On the one hand, there is out-and-out repression. It ranges from expulsion to genocide, depending on how the regime defines its enemies. Usually the rules are even cast in paper. But in other cases, the officials in charge take informal action, especially where foreigners are concerned. A correspondent is refused accreditation, a troublesome contemporary historian doesn't have his visa renewed. The visitor's hotel room is searched. Manuscripts are confiscated at the frontier. A breach of foreign exchange control regulations can have unpleasant consequences. Mild forms of blackmail are also available to them.

Often it's enough to have friends who are suspected of heresy; or some spy happens to report coarse remarks about the ruling number one. That earns the foreigner the status for which Cuban officialdom has the lovely word *conflictivo*. Translated into diplomatic language that means you become *persona non grata*. It's not threatening. No arrest, no deportation, just some minor harassment now and then, a tiny privilege that disappears, a little more surveillance. I don't know what was the final straw in our case. Was it the Padilla Affair? Was it something I'd published in Europe? Or did we fall into disfavour when the *Máximo líder* praised the Soviet invasion of Czechoslovakia? Was it really only at that point that we realized it was better to pack our bags in Havana?

Once you were back in your comfortable house in Berlin what did things look like there?

I found an old wardrobe that was crammed with mail. Normal correspondence wasn't possible between Berlin and Havana. You had to rely on go-betweens, couriers, messengers who'd smuggle the occasional manuscript or parcel past customs or the censors. Otherwise we were practically cut of from correspondence by post. For that reason a woman who lived nearby had put everything that arrived for me in that wardrobe. Most of it was no longer relevant anyway. We are more dispensable than we like to think.

Surely you must have brought some things back from Havana? Show me your souvenirs.

A machete, brand name Crowing Cock, with a 60cm handle, made in China. Polaroids that have long since faded. A frock coat, made by Franz Winter, Braunau i. B. before the First World War. Rolls of film in a metal box. An album from the Consejo Nacional de Cultura containing marvellous examples of artwork —allegories of pleasure and wealth, gold printed stickers for cigar boxes with crowns, medals, buxom ladies with rosy butcher's-wife cheeks representing Ceres and Industria, the goddesses of tillage and manufacture. *Qualité somptueuse*! In a tin there's a miniature model of the cruiser *Aurora*. And then there's a silk, paisley-patterned Indian wrapover jacket, never worn; on the label it says: Burlington's Ashoka Hotel, New Delhi. Cambodian coins, rouble notes, Hong Kong dollars. A brown, crumbling 2-peso banknote that was never worth very much, signed by Ernesto Guevara de la Serna, Head of the National Bank of Cuba—by him of all people who could never handle money! This residue is like a Sargasso Sea on dry land.

———

Did you sometimes dream of Cuba?

Of course. I just can't say why I've found it so difficult to free myself of that little, insignificant, crazy island.

That's all you have to tell me?

Yes, 1968—by now that's nothing more than an imaginary date, a teeming mass of reminiscences, delusions, generalizations and projections that has taken the place of the things that had happened during these few years. My experiences are buried under the dungheap of the media, archive material, panel discussions, experiences stylized the way war veterans do and that are now beyond imagining.

I presume a summary is beyond you?

My dear chap, you know as well as I do that the tumult is never-ending. It just goes on somewhere else, in Mogadishu, in Damascus, in Lagos or in Kiev, in all those places where we are fortunate enough not to live. It's just a question of perspective.

That sounds conciliatory.

I hope not. I never wanted to become someone like you. Fortunately, we're pretty unlike each other.

At least that's something we can agree on.

In the autumn of 1969 a messenger, whose name I have forgotten, delivered two mailbags with material from Kommune 1, that had finally broken up after squatting in an abandoned factory in Moabit for several months. I wasn't surprised to find box files with neatly glued-in newspaper cuttings in them. All that orderliness was presumably connected with the fact that the members of the group attached great importance to the media response to their activities. I passed the two bags on to a place where people are interested in such bequests—the Instituut voor Sociale Geschiedenis in Amsterdam.

Anyone who wants to know more about the members of the Kommune can look at my brother's book: Ulrich Enzensberger, *Die Jahre der Kommune 1: Berlin, 1967–1969* (Cologne: Kiepenheuer & Witsch, 2004).

Long after I had left, the protest movement also arrived in Middletown. In the summer of 1970, Wesleyan University had to close down because the students were blocking all the lectures. Many of the professors showed solidarity with them as well.

My journey around the world was, as Imre Kertesz put it in his 2011–12 journals, 'futile, exhausting but marvellous.'

A selection of Heberto Padilla's poems has also appeared in German in 1971: *Außerhalb des Spiels*, translated from the Spanish by Günter Maschke. In English: *Sent off the Field: A Selection from the Poetry of Heberto Padilla* (1974), translated by J. M. Cohen.

An earlier, lesser version of 'My Memories of the Tumult' was printed to accompany an exhibition in Nuremberg: *Hommage à Jiří Kolář. Tagebuch 1968* (Kunssthalle Nürnberg, 1984), pp. 10–11.

Ach Europa! is the title of a book that was published in 1987. I mention it here because Jiří Kolář contributed collages for the cover and endpaper. He died in Prague in 2002.

Haydée Santamaría shot herself in her office in July 1980, a suicide that was extremely embarrassing for the regime. Not long before that Castro had called everyone who didn't agree with him 'scum', and called on them to leave the country. Thereupon 125,000 people, who didn't need to be asked twice, left the island from Mariel Harbour in a flotilla of small boats, heading for Florida. That was the beginning of a 'grey decade'. Haydée lost support and saw no future for her work. Perhaps, she was just taking a line from the Cuban national anthem literally: 'To die for your country is to live.'

Arthur Lehning saw the first day of the twenty-first century. He died in Lys-Saint-Georges on 1 January 2000, his hundredth birthday. A translation of his *Unterhaltungen mit Bakunin* (Conversations with Bakunin) was published in 1987 by Greno, Nördlingen.

'Calm were the northern evenings . . . ' A few lines from 'Erinnerung an die sechziger Jahre' (Remembering the 1960s) in *Blindenschrift* (Braille) published in 1964.

Carlos Franqui died in Puerto Rico in 2010, still unreconciled.

There is a lot about Nelly Sachs in a wonderful album that Aris Fioretos published to accompany an exhibition 40 years after her death in 2012: *Nelly Sachs, Flight and Metamorphosis*, orig. *Flucht und Verwandlung*.

The only people who can explain the frenzy to which I submitted both externally and internally are astrologists, who are never short of reasons. In fact, in 1968, there was an extremely rare conjunction of Pluto and Uranus. Both were in opposition to Saturn. Bingo!

After my return I wrote a few lines about the difficulties of re-education:

Simply splendid
all these grand plans:
the Golden Age
the Kingdom of God on earth
the withering away of the state.
Makes sense.

If it wasn't for people!
People are always getting in the way.
They mess everything up.

When the liberation of mankind is at stake
they go off to the barber's.
Instead of trotting along enthusiastically
    behind the advance guard
they say: I quite fancy a beer now.
Instead of for the just cause,
they're fighting against varicose veins and
    measles.
At the decisive moment
they're looking for a letter box or a bed.
Just as the millennium's about to dawn
they're boiling up nappies.

People spoil everything.
You can't build anything on them.
Every one of them's a spanner in the works.

Petty-bourgeois shilly-shallying!
Consumer idiots!
Leftovers from the past!
You can't just kill off the lot of 'em.
You can't spend the whole day going on at 'em.
Yes, if it wasn't for people,
then things would look very different.

Yes, if it wasn't for people
then it would take no time at all.
Yes, if it wasn't for people
Yes, then!
(Then I won't trouble you any longer either.)

A kind of purgatory. One day it was all over. 'I don't know why, but I'm overcome with a great sense of calm.' When I wrote those two lines, the period of normalization had begun. Had reason returned? No. But the tumult had not been in vain. It depends on what it produced in the long run. Not just for me but also for the vast majority, even for those who had nothing to do with it.

For to my surprise—very gradually, almost behind our backs—our desolate country was becoming more and more a land that was fit to live in. No one clicked their heels any more, no one bowed and scraped, drivers started to let pedestrians go first at crossings, the police cast off their military-style shakos, bus conductors waited for old ladies instead of driving off just as they reached the stop. The pandering law stating that *anyone* facilitating sexual contact between unmarried couples was liable to prosecution was abolished and homosexuality decriminalized. Against the delaying resistance of the authoritarian state more relaxed manners gained acceptance. Wonders never ceased in Germany. You got the impression the Federal Republic was on the way to becoming civilized.

It was time to say farewell to the political and private obsessions that had haunted me during the past few years. In order to achieve a minimum of clarity about them I went so far—I could also say, sank so low—as to keep a confused diary for a few months, confident that if the writer should read them at a later date, such notes would fill him with the revulsion they deserve. We'll see each other again, I thought. And I was right. Here are a few excerpts from those pages:

First of all, the political situation: The Grand Arrangement is making progress. In Germany, the Brandt administration is defusing the confrontation at the Wall with their new policy towards Eastern Europe. There is talk of amnesties for the APO, the so-called Extra-Parliamentary Opposition.

But the mortally ill poet is still sitting in his kitchen in Prague, typing out the book that will never be printed. As ever, the spies are standing outside his house. In the dilapidated brewery, Václav Havel is leaning on the beer barrels in his dirty rubber apron. And Dubček is carrying his worn briefcase to the office of a hopeless forestry commission.

New deals between the great powers are on the agenda. Nixon is preparing for his journey to Peking and giving up his attempt to isolate China. The Soviet Union, an 'Upper Volta with rockets', brought to the edge of paralysis by the difficulties it only has itself to blame for, is sounding out agreements with the USA. Even the Cuban conflict has been put on ice. It can only be a matter of time before the lost war in Vietnam will end by mutual agreement. Soon Le Duc Tho, the leader of the North Vietnam Communist Party, and my favourite war criminal, Henry Kissinger, will be able to share the Nobel Peace Prize.

Why not? What we have here is peace. Goods are multiplying like rabbits. All the goods here are of peacetime quality, the people as well. There's even something civilian about the politicians. The emergency laws are fading away in a drawer. At summit meetings there's talk of non-aggression pacts. Since 1945 we've been let off History; on leave from the front. Never was it more idyllic behind the lines, the summer more carefree.

You can't argue with these appearances. We're not surprised that the house doesn't blow up. The war's happening somewhere else. Sometimes the word *Ussuri* appears in the newspaper, but who knows what that river's called in Chinese?

Can things go on like this? At least the end-of-season sale should give us pause for thought. The electric clock on the table isn't ticking any more. It works silently. Progress again! Of course, inside my head I know what's going on. But I simply can't manage to feel afraid. There's iced melon for afters. In the past we fought in a different way.

Some raise their index finger in triumph and say they'd seen it all coming. It's so satisfying to be right for once, even if it took decades! Others still believe in Mao and put their money on China, where the red day is dawning, just as Vladimir and Estragon waited for Godot, or they see the last beacon of the International in Enver Hoxha. Anyone who talks about the revolution as if it were just around the corner knows less about politics than a chimney sweep who's on the council of a small town in Bavaria.

A limited company. When, in 1970, it was no longer possible to continue with Suhrkamp, the periodical *Kursbuch* had to find a new partner. It was Klaus Wagenbach who was prepared to put the facilities of his small publishing house at our disposal. But I knew the comrades among our readers well enough to be aware that they saw the ugly face of profit peeking out from behind even the most modest of firms. In order to forestall this suspicion we had to make sure we never paid out even the smallest dividend.

To start with, we set up a limited company. To do that we had to go through rituals I knew nothing about—files full of contracts, the idiotic solemnity of legal declarations, all sorts of linguistic contortions, being entered in the register of companies and opening an account at the bank. Like one of Pavlov's dogs, the branch manager was exposed to two contrary signals at the same time: suspicion and the prospect of gaining new customers.

Bourgeois legislation makes heavy weather of preventing the accumulation of capital in the hands of partners. It turns a blind eye as long as no one raises a complaint against you. Our intention to secure the magazine against political pressure was considered irrelevant. Wagenbach and I found ourselves forced into the role of benefactors who, however, could at any time take a much tougher approach if they felt like it.

As it turned out, it was not at all easy to expropriate oneself.

You may! I'm checking out. You could put it that way. I'm afraid my feverish interest in politics was always just self-defence. Weren't there things in the world that were more important than the tedious, repetitive, eternal struggle for power?

In July 1970 I went with Tanaquil to Provence for a few weeks. We'd made a habit of going away together once every year. This had nothing to do with my other travels. It was my daughter who decided where we should go. This time she wanted to go to France. We visited our old friend Roger Pillaudin in Lauris.

When we were still in the bloom of youth, he'd taught me a few things that were new to me in the dire 1950s. Not only did he know Alfred Jarry's *Ubu Roi*, could quote whole verses of Apollinaire by heart, and introduced me to Queneau and Ionesco, he convinced me of his motto for life and that was: You may! In the provincial Germany of the times, immured in taboos, that was an unthinkable idea. To my innocent eyes, Paris looked as if it were the quintessential city of light and Roger's little attic flat in Belleville was for many years my refuge from the excessive demands that my own country made on me. Neither of us had any money but Roger came from the Auvergne and refused to compromise as far as food was concerned. He wrote poems, had no success with them, earned his living with a job in broadcasting and became a genius in the medium. Then he got fed up with living in Paris, he didn't like the climate, and moved to Provence.

The doors of his spacious house were open all day. On the patio people would gather for pastis and a chat—musicians, dancers and people who in some unspecified way worked in the theatre, radio or for small publishers: a second-hand bookseller, who rarely opened his shop; the wife of a Cambridge don; a young lad who designed knitting patterns or a Russian they called 'Grand Duke' who had been happily living above his means for years. The farmers' sons from the village also felt at home there. These people couldn't care less about politics. That gave them an aura of freedom you didn't get in Berlin.

Heiner, a fabulous dancer from Düsseldorf with a liver disorder, homosexual and incapable of abstraction, drove us to Avignon in his little car. There you could meet Jean Vilar in the Civette while a clown was trying to sell the thoughts of Mao Tse-tung to desperate tourists stumbling out of the Papal Palace into the open air with handkerchiefs over their heads. In the evening there was art everywhere. It's simply ineradicable down there.

The next day we drove on to Aix, where Henze's *El Cimarrón* happened to be on. Stom, the Japanese percussionist, was an adherent of Zen Buddhism, while on Cours Mirabeau the singer Leo Brower, in his green shirt, was worried about the Cuban revolution. He was besieged by stupid, harmless girls who had nothing else in their minds than to spend an hour between the sheets with him. There were always new things in the boutiques: the safari look, brass studded belts, Indian shirts in hand-woven voile.

Afterwards, there was a village ball behind the *mairie*, the town hall, that Roger had organized. Fat Simone brought chilled punch made from orange juice and rum. Four serious black Cubans played their music from the Havana bars. José Martí and 'Guantanamera' again, but please, no politics. Tanaquil, 13 and in her first ball gown, bought in Aix the previous day ('*cela s'appelle un smock*,' with a pleated waist, puffed sleeves, pink and almost transparent), danced salsa with the Japanese dervish. I found the sawdust under my feet more convincing than all the mudbath into which the Berlin movement had sunk.

On our journey home we visited Diego Camacho in Choisy-le-Roi. He was a Spanish émigré who, mostly at night or on Sundays, was working on the biography of Buenaventura Durruti, a hero of the Spanish Civil War. On weekdays he was occupied in a little workshop, where the old anarchists printed not just cinema posters or invitations to masked balls but also their own leaflets and brochures. He invited us to olives and ham in his small apartment. In a good half hour on the Metro one could be outside the town house of Baroness Rothschild, who used to invite all the left-wingers of Paris to dinner and, so it was said, admired my poems.

The Havana Inquiry. I've even been to Reckling-hausen once. At first sight this town in the Ruhr has nothing to do with the battle at the Bay of Pigs in Cuba in 1961. It was already 12 years ago that the CIA attempted an armed invasion there with Kennedy's backing. When it failed, Castro's army took more than a thousand prisoners, and the USA had to pay over 60 million dollars in ransom to free their mercenaries.

The place where all this happened, the Bay of Pigs, is not very impressive. There is absolutely nothing to see there, not even piglets. Despite that I went back to the military operation. I even wrote a book about it. It was called: *The Havana Inquiry: A Self Portrait of the Counter-Revolution*. The cover was done in green and brown camouflage colours.

Since I had nothing better to do in Havana, while I was there I went to the TV studios where I watched the recordings from April 1961 and wrote down what had happened. The victors had arranged a public hearing of their prisoners that lasted four nights. It was a fairly unique process, allowing the prisoners on the stage to explain their motives and defend themselves. It's rare for a dictatorship to allow such a risky discussion with its enemies.

Eventually I imported that event to Reckling-hausen, a place that is pretty far away from Havana. The West German Broadcasting Corporation was involved, the performance was supported by the Ruhr Festival and the Essen Theatre. The director was Müller-Stahl, Münchenhagen played the presenter and the whole thing was broadcast live. It wasn't an exotic spectacle from the Caribbean that I had in mind but an experimental set-up. I wanted to put a German double beside each of the Cubans who had been interrogated. That wasn't easy because among the invaders were the sons of corrupt politicians, men from the secret service, a torturer and an army chaplain as well as ordinary people and harmless reformists. Some counterparts were easy to find: expropriated landowners from East Prussia who wanted their estates back, the daughter of a German politician who was known for his corruption, even a pastor from the armed forces was prepared to appear. A two-hour TV drama like that could easily have gone wrong, on the one hand because the parallels were not always convincing, and on the other because the German guests put up as good a fight as their Cuban counterparts had done in the past. It was a risky affair, much more exciting than a talk show. In those days something like that was still possible on German TV.

Poor sexologists. N. is half Brazilian, half French; she has no occupation. Her money comes partly from her parents, who earn enough for a comfortable old age in the shrinking colonial empire, and partly from her men. She lives in Paris, travels a lot, is generous, carefree and forgetful. She only takes notice of misfortune when it concerns one of her friends, but then she helps them with what she has without hesitation. I was happy to let myself be seduced by her. There is an animal strength to her lovemaking but not a trace of tenderness.

That it is easier to take off one's clothes than to expose one's feelings is part of the discretion of the south. Those of a northern disposition find that difficult to understand. They feel hurt when a woman manages without the lies civilization expects of her.

How stupid the studies of women's sexuality are! The research done à la Kinsey & Masters confuses the inhabitants of American suburbs with humanity in general. In that way sex education becomes mystification, therapy propaganda. An Andalusian woman will hardly let the curve of her climax be determined by such specialists.

A lover such as N. can give a man refreshments, massage him, without it ever occurring to her that such simple actions could be interpreted as symbols of oppression. Every sign of independence in lovemaking is also liberating for the man. There is great fascination in a woman who is free from the halitosis of sentimentality.

Old photographs. In one of my drawers there are pictures of friends who have since gone grey, houses from my childhood days and girls I never fucked. There's a photo of an unknown woman which is a mystery to me. On the back, written in tiny handwriting like that of an old woman, is: 'Agosto 1951. Isla de la Virgen del Mar'.

On the photo is a beautiful, very calm-looking woman. She has a parting in her long black hair and a scarf covering the back of her neck. He dress is also dark and is pleated like that of a statue of the Madonna. She has white lace over her breast and shoulders. You can see the base of her neck, her collar-bones and her arms, that are bare up to the armpit.

The woman is lying on a rock in the sea, the surf can be seen behind it. She's leaning on her elbow. Her face, that of a 27-year-old, is quite motionless. She's not looking at the photographer. Perhaps she's unaware of his presence. She's gazing at the water. It looks as if she's listening to something or musing on something far away. Her fingers, splayed out on the rock, seem somewhat podgy, but her features are finely drawn. Her feet, hidden by her dress and the rock, cannot be seen. She looks very much alone. It's not a posed picture.

In 1951 I couldn't speak a word of Spanish. Even today I don't know where the Isla de la Virgen del Mar is. The photo is printed on what specialists call *chamois* paper, and the edges are cut in that unpleasant regular–irregular way, that was still fashionable in the 1950s. There's a yellow blotch on the lower right-hand corner. I've never seen this woman. Never will her gaze rest on me. All she sees is the rock and the water. All works of art are like her, they share a promise that is never kept.

Herr Gustafsson in person. You have to have patience to get from Oslo to Dunshammar in Västmanland by rail, but to make up for it once you're there you're surrounded by a peacefulness that's impossible to imagine anywhere else. Lars Gustafsson, with his wife Madeleine, who was probably cleverer than he was but kept that to herself, often used to retire to his modest house in Åmänningen for the summer.

He himself was more surprised than anyone at his inspired ideas. He played little pieces on the flute and used to moan about social democracy. All that gave us time enough to go through a couple of translations that I'd made of his precise, mysterious poems. (Someone once called Lars a 'rationalist mystic', a characterization that makes sense.)

We went rowing on the deep, treacherous lake and talked about Frege, Wittgenstein and the finds from the Iron Age—1,500 years ago, the people here dug up the ore from the ground, made kilns out of clay and stone, and brought the iron to sintering point at over a thousand degrees. In the woods we passed a white villa. From the open window a sonata by Johan Helmich Roman could be heard. A soft breeze ruffled the curtain. I would have liked to see the woman playing the piano but she stayed out of sight.

A couple of times I also visited Lars in Västerås. He is one of the last of the Swedish mandarins. His disarming vanity, like his mental agility, reveals his training in the schools of Uppsala and Oxford. We amused ourselves by nominating the worst classics. Lars: Rubens. I: Dostoyevsky. He: Balzac. As a prime example of a bad classic I proposed Wagner who, of course, is a classic and will remain so. Otherwise the game wouldn't work.

We both agreed that, like children, what we liked about pictures was what was in them. The disaster that is abstract painting—it shows nothing but states of mind, but we know those anyway. Or avant-garde literature that contains nothing but itself. In music as well, the more advanced it is, the less there is to hear. That 'ordinary people' stick to trashy novels and kitschy pictures has its reasons. In a certain sense, the *Stag at Bay* represents needs that are denied by contemporary art.

But my friend Lars does not correspond to the cliché of the absent-minded scholar. He loves working with tools, he polishes stones, mends fishing nets and once even sunk a well. That perhaps comes from the fact that his parents weren't well off. His father just about managed to make ends meet as an insurance agent during the 1920s and 30s. His mother, a friendly woman, turned in on herself, with no hopes for the future, is a little strange in the head and doesn't read her son's books.

Nelly Sachs died in May 1970. She had entrusted me with the task of looking after her works, so I had to go to Stockholm to deal with her literary estate. Alone the task would have been beyond me, but with the help of her good friends, Bengt and Margaretha Holmqvist, at least I managed to sort some things out.

Two nice kids. Two years ago they were still hanging around with friends, swallowing LSD; they had no money but always the latest records and projects for this or that film. Now they're both working in a factory and have joined 'the ML', that is, one of the three pro-Chinese sects here in the city. There are lots of these abbreviations. They know them by heart and can distinguish between them just as easily as the brand names of cigarettes or cars. In Berlin there are newspapers that keep track of them and call on people to join campaigns. Three people in a room decide, 'Everyone to the Ruhr' or 'Smash the Bundeswehr'. They call on their supporters to get married, to abstain from birth control and to have enough children that the world will soon be populated with Marxist–Leninists.

Like all those who have joined such an organization, they always talk about their own party in the singular, if they're asked which party they don't quite understand the question. Even after the second split the 'Party' remains the only one there can be. They talk about the latest resolutions of the Central Committee with a kind of yearning, demand purges and are outraged at the threat of proceedings brought against them by the Party. They enjoy using the words 'glorious' or 'heroic'. The earnestness with which they discuss the arguments among the leadership— that is half a dozen comrades—is touching. They have bizarre respect for the Trotskyites who, they say, know how to undermine the Party and infiltrate its committees. Naturally there are only a couple of dozen members of the Fourth International in Berlin, but those people are 'objectively' agents of imperialism. The young woman confided in me that under her pillow she has a book entitled 'The Great Conspiracy' that doesn't mince words in unmasking that gang.

For all that this couple are simply nice. The two of them have given up their habits and their comfort, and, as far as possible, deny their background, for the sake of the 'cause'. The workers have no reason to be frightened of them. That is good to hear, for if a revolution really were on the agenda and that kind of nice semi-lunatics had a say in the matter, there would be only one option for the people—to dash off, screaming, to find a place where they are safe from so much blindness.

Personal matters. A.'s girlfriend is furious. He suggested she read a piece by Lenin. 'Always this same old boring rubbish,' she screams. After a quarrel that goes on all night, she leaves him. B.'s wife asks his publisher not to put a picture of the author on the jacket: 'You know how ugly he is.' Why does C. take five sleeping pills every evening? No one knows why comrade D. killed himself. F. maintains with impunity that his thesis is the most significant Marxist text that has appeared in Germany since Walter Benjamin. Why did G. not tell his girlfriend that he has a dose of the clap? Does H. always have to tell his guests how much the wine he's pouring them cost? The last play I. directs is torn to pieces by all the reviewers. He suffers a heart attack but has over a 100,000 marks in his account.

The names are interchangeable. Gossip provides more precise information on the Left in Berlin than any analysis of imperialism. There is no conclusive answer to the question of why anyone should voluntarily subject themselves to such a compulsively neurotic environment.

A strange meeting on an aeroplane. Beside me there's a tradesman who's on his third beer. He wants to chat. It's no good in the East, he explains, but in the West as well life has no meaning any more. Actually he would most like to have been a forester because it's better out in the countryside. The point of the story: it turns out that he's the son of the writer Ernst Jünger. He defends his father, in a good-natured but rather clueless way, against his enemies.

Many people of my age are mesmerized by their date of birth. Is their body starting to let the down already? Fantasies and fears of impotence. Before breakfast they contemplate their hairbrush with horror because there are a few strands of hair left in it. But even a hardliner fritters away his time, cleans his teeth, fills in forms and goes to the barber's.

Reading instead of amphetamines. Political periodicals and magazines keep going over the same old things again and again, often in abstract theoretical terms. One is called *Marxist Digest*—the theory is beginning to consume itself. I also lack the patience for new literary works.

Dear old Montaigne. Leafing back and forth in a life that, despite the historical distance, seems less alien. The surprising thing is the incredible freshness of the middle-class consciousness at work in him.

Or *Bouvard et Pécuchet*. Flaubert's hatred is directed less at stupidity itself than at his conclusion that reality shows stupidity to be right. It's quite clear that he recognized himself in his two fictional writers. He didn't know that when he started the book. A blind spot is inevitable when you undertake something like that. It can make your mind reel when a stupid sentence turns out to be true: 'Money alone can't make you happy.'—'Get a job first, then you can demonstrate.'—'You've never loved me.'

Shaken by the banality, you cling on to your chair, as you do in an aeroplane when it gets into an air pocket.

The third secular saint I cling on to is Diderot. They ought to make *Jacques le fataliste* into a film. The structure of that masterpiece anticipates the montage technique of film anyway. Location: the Cévennes, the Massif Central; regions almost entirely unpopulated. The two heroes move across the mountains and plateaus like figures in a ballet. Their clothes torn, their three-cornered hats moth-eaten, their horses all skin and bone. All in greys and browns, no bright colours. The shabbiness and poverty of the provinces in the eighteenth century. There is a sediment of pessimism beneath the brightness of the narrative, of despair beneath the gallows humour. Scenes that aren't in the book ought to be introduced, just as in the background of Brueghel's paintings, a woman is being raped here, a house set on fire there, without the main figures taking any notice.

Irrespective of such a plan, I decide to read that story again once every year.

Visitors from California. Hardly anyone could be more German that Reinhard Lettau. He comes from Thuringia and claims that Erfurt is the centre of the Earth. But at the same time he left his home country. He preferred to live as an émigré and was proud of his American passport. A writer such as him is a rarity in Germany. He doesn't produce a lot but never writes anything that is really poor. It was only two years ago that he published his splendid book *Enemies* that is worth a whole hundredweight of political pamphlets and pirated copies. He's a militant, but in his own way. For him to be radical is not least a question of style. Instead of trotting along in demonstrations or throwing stones at the Springer Building, he preferred to tear the Springer tabloid, *Bildzeitung*, to pieces in front of the TV cameras.

Not long ago the Lettaus came back to Berlin. Hardly are the two of them sitting at my table, drinking tea and greeting a piece of camembert with cries of delight, handing over their presents, experiences and words—(*it's really something else, why, it's something out of space*)—than the city on the front line is changing, has a less narrow-minded, a virtually aristocratic look about it. You forgive him his absurd outbreaks of revulsion when he calls everything he doesn't like 'fascist', whether it's an annoying wasp or the ugly facade of the house opposite. Reinhard's grace, his politeness and his wit turn his visit into an unexpected joy.

His wife, Veronique, has returned from the USA a completely changed woman. Previously she was naive and confused, now she knows exactly what she wants. When she has a drink, smokes a pipe or reads a book, she always asks herself, 'What will the bosses say about this?' If the bosses are pleased, that's bad, if they're annoyed, that's good. So she shares the paranoia of the left-wingers, though only in a mild way. We can presumably assume that the bosses couldn't care less what Véronique drinks or what books she reads. The advantage of having a simple view of the world outweighs any objections.

Her Party, that only appears in the singular, calls itself 'Progressive Labour'. At the beginning, Véronique says, she had the odd problem with Party resolutions that didn't seem to make sense to her but she'd hit on a way of overcoming her doubts. The best way, she said, was to defend the rituals, that were difficult for her to understand, when talking to other people. In this way you ended up finding that you were convinced yourself. Thus, the childlike Véro rediscovered Pascal's maxim that you can reach belief through the outward signs of belief.

The Bernina Express. A visit to Herbert Marcuse who's spending his holidays at the Kronenhof in Pontresina. The town could have been invented by Dürrenmatt, full of rhododendrons, young ladies and cuckoo clocks. With his upper-class manner the philosopher fitted in very well. Swiss luxury has always been plain and simple, solid and inexorable. The visitors who are there for their health, average age 60, in knee-breeches and anorak, armed with walking sticks, do the so-called fitness trail—that is a path through the woods plastered with enamel signs. Every few minutes you can read the instructions for some gymnastic exercise on them. Marcuse, who is very keen on doing his walks, replies, with the calmest expression in the world, to the cheerful greetings of the German couples, 'After you.'

A conversation with him shows that, miles away from any opportunism, he holds on to his ideas with appealing obstinacy. Ultimately they can be traced back to the traditions of German idealism. His suspicion of ordinary people is boundless. He only uses the word *proletariat* in ironic inverted commas, maintaining that the alternative, *das Volk*, is a Nazi concept. The man who was writing about the repressive character of culture 30 years ago, retains a belief in art that I find almost bizarre—Goethe's *Faust*, he says, contains more revolutionary potential than all the political cadres of the Western world. He may not be wrong in that. But I find his stubbornness so provoking that I'm eventually transformed into a shy Leninist defending the dictatorship of the proletariat against Plato's rule of the philosophers. Thus both of us end up barking up the wrong tree in the middle of the Swiss forest.

Idées fixes. My difficulties with religions, philosophies and ideological systems—unfortunately, I can never quite believe that they're meant seriously. When someone tells me that my dislike of barbers comes from a fear of castration, they just make me laugh. Clearly there is supposed to be something else behind everything I perceive, and that something else is what is true. Of course I've never 'seriously' believed in the existence of a world spirit. An epistemologist has assured me that there is no definite answer to the question of whether the world outside actually exists. Well, well.

Perhaps trapped inside every general theory there's a bottle imp that can't wait to escape. But I don't know the magic word that would liberate the demon. Let it stay where it is, whatever it's called: class position or Holy Ghost, the being of beings or instinctual structures.

The hypothesis that there are no individuals any more, that the core of a person has become mere outward show, is very popular. It's easy to see what's right about it. Yet I feel sorry for anyone who takes it at face value and swallows it whole. That can lead to an urge to cough and difficulty in breathing. Alienation or not, everyone can tell other people apart, and not just by their names or caps, but by their gait, their voice, even by the noises they make when they put the kettle on in the kitchen. Everyone knows that, but many don't dare contradict the dogmas that have been drummed into them. 'Repressive tolerance', 'the terror of consumerism', 'manipulation' are all heuristic concepts that can be useful in certain situations but should be thrown away after use.

But the way left-wing people are today, they're so in thrall to their dogmas that they'd rather ignore the plainest evidence than chuck their *idées fixes* into the wastepaper basket. Sometimes even Liberation comes trotting along in a corset.

A blank sheet. Armand Gatti has a story about a journey to Peking. A group of visitors from Europe is introduced to Mao Tse-tung. Each of them has the opportunity to ask him a question and Gatti wants to know how the Great Chairman sees the future. Mao takes a notebook out of his breast pocket, leafs through it until he finds a blank page, tears it out and hands it to Gatti.

Gatti kept the white sheet of paper for months between the pages of a book. One day his children took the book off the shelf, found the piece of paper and covered it with coloured hieroglyphs that defied all attempts to decipher them.

Another farewell to Cuba. Heberto Padilla was arrested in March 1971, accused of 'subversive activities against the government'. It came to a show trial at which he was forced to make a humiliating confession. These proceedings, that recalled the Moscow trials of 1936, attracted worldwide attention. Twenty-six authors, among them Jean-Paul Sartre, Julio Cortázar, Italo Calvino, Carlos Fuentes, Marguerite Duras, Juan and Luis Goytisolo, Alberto Moravia, Jorge Semprún, Susan Sontag, Pier Paolo Pasolini, Juan Rulfo and Mario Vargas Llosa sent an open letter to Castro to which the ruler responded with an outburst of rage. The writers, he said, were 'bourgeois intellectuals, slanderers and agents of the CIA, imperialist spies, to whom entry to Cuba would be refused now and for ever.' That was stupid and cost him and his regime what was left of the esteem among left-wingers in the West. From then on I too was, of course, counted among the agents of imperialism because I was one of the first to sign the letter. Welcome to the club!

An evening with burnt children. The president invites a number of Latin American authors to visit the Federal Republic. The official in charge draws up a programme that hardly differs from those the Soviets offer their delegations. There are the usual little vouchers for breakfast and dinner, endless coach journeys to see Holstein cows or a car factory. Time is made for interviews, colloquia and receptions as well. The composition of the delegation is odd. The participants make every effort to be polite, but the Padilla Affair is smouldering in the background. Worse are other political differences. An ashen-complexioned secretary from Argentina seems to represent the military dictatorship. Three Brazilians are strikingly reticent. But there are also a few stars among them: Mario Vargas Llosa and Gabriel García Márquez, old acquaintances and rivals who carry on their arguments with caustic humour.

As I can speak a little Spanish, I suggest we have a relaxing evening at my place and a dozen of the visitors actually accept my invitation. There's enough to drink. Literature is the topic we talk about least. After an hour, as if by arrangement, the bores, among them Asturias, who can't get rid of the stigma of the Nobel Prize, get up and leave. The music's turned up, a joint is passed around, some lie down on the floor. They're all relieved. For a few hours they've escaped the programme.

Incidental expenses. It is said of many so-called sixty-eighters that they made comfortable careers for themselves. Most of them only made it as far as professors or teachers, state employees on permanent contracts with pension rights. You can probably count those who became ministers, permanent secretaries and important figures in the economy on the fingers of both hands. But there has never been a political movement without people going to the dogs. Often they were people who were unselfish in more than one sense—they showed no consideration either for themselves or for others, and often dragged their unsuspecting followers down with them. For a few their downfall brought a dubious posthumous fame. Transfigured by the media they became martyrs or pop icons.

Most of them were soon forgotten. No one mentions the names of those who ended up mired in drugs, in prison or in a mental hospital. Not a few of them killed themselves.

As I withdrew, that for me actually meant gaining more freedom, I often thought of those losers. During the years of the tumult, I was occasionally seen as playing an active role in which I was genuinely never interested. But I couldn't, and still can't, deny that I have some sense of being part of it. Everyone who was involved in the chaos feels more or less responsible. So I see what I can do to help a few of those unknown persons or, where that isn't possible, remember them.

I count everyone as part of that, no matter which side they were on; even the labourer Josef Baumann, who was sentenced to seven years in prison for attempted murder and who hung himself in his cell, as well as Dutschke, whom he tried to kill and who drowned in his bath in Denmark nine years later. Radicalism knows no mercy.

Prospects for the hereafter. The Muslims' paradise promises the faithful the things real life denies them: green meadows instead of the desert sand; beautiful houris instead of inaccessible women and homosexuality out of necessity; rich food that dissolves into thin air instead of threatening them with diarrhoea or cholera. As a precise negation of social reality, this paradise follows a stringent logic.

Christianity has two paradises that in a strange way compete with each other. The Garden of Eden derives from an old oriental fantasy. It is sensuous and is described in visual terms: luxuriant vegetation, the people are naked, in harmony with nature, they don't have to work. In contrast to that, the heavenly paradise is controlled by the pure doctrine of a ban on images that paralyses the imagination and promises nothing but eternal boredom. In Europe the fear of hell was always stronger than the desire for such a reward. Thus the catechism defeats itself with its own weapons and religion gives birth to neurosis.

In earlier years I was even scandalized by the Garden of Eden. As a child it seemed to me that a paradise with signs such as 'Don't spit on the ground', 'Dogs must be kept on a lead' and 'Eating apples is forbidden' didn't deserve that name. Today I see it differently, for with the ban the inhabitants were also given freedom and time—the time before and the time after. The apple was the greatest pleasure the Garden had to offer. It released the trapdoor, the emergency exit, promised physical love and intelligence. Without the forbidden fruit, the place would have been a prison. One requirement of a paradise is that you can leave it when you've had enough. That is also true of political paradises such as the one promised by communism.

Silence is golden. My brother Christian tells me about the sick, ugly, half-crazy poet R. who left the GDR and lives on some kind of small pension. She was always strange, a latecomer; her writings were bedside-table mysticism. But Christian says she had her moments. As when, scurrying around the kitchen, she says, with the innocence only a poetess can manage, 'So better dead than in the proletariat.'

This statement, one of the most frequent thoughts of the century, is never brought up during a political discussion. But most of those sitting on the platform express it with every sip they take from their glass and with every button on their shirt. Most communists I know would find it impossible to admit that.

Anyone working on an assembly line is more likely to be saying to himself, 'I'd rather be alive than where I am.' They call that 'bourgeoisification'. There is nothing they object to more in a worker. Left-wingers shout 'petty bourgeois' all the more often the closer they are to that class themselves, and the more they immerse themselves in class analysis, the less it occurs to them to apply it to themselves. If they did, it would reveal conditions that contradict everything their theory teaches. So they have to keep the things they propagate as far away from themselves as possible.

Talking about the Gulliver complex. A fright from my early years that I've never entirely got over. It must have been when I was five that I read Swift for the first time, in one of the standard expurgated editions. In the book there was a colourful, crude but precisely drawn illustration. A giant was lying in a field. He was tethered down by a lot of thin strings and couldn't move, even though he was stronger than the Lilliputians, who were standing around him, grinning; for they were many and acted in unison.

Why did I, like most children, immediately identify with Gulliver? It was as if I could feel the threads
on my own skin, the pain of the bonds, the tempta-
tion to tear myself free by force, yes, even the irony
that lay in the fact that the victim was torturing himself, so to speak. After all, he could just lie there, still
and resigned.

But there's more that becomes apparent in this
picture than I'm happy with. Do I resemble this
intruder who's forced his way into the Empire of
Lilliput all alone? Why don't I see myself as one of
the company of dwarves that embodies a social ratio-
nale? What is the megalomania that makes a five-year-
old feel like a giant?

What was it that finally did for Heine, that stubborn man who held his head high right to the end, as
if he knew nothing of the bonds pressing down on
him? They were very different threads than mine
and much stronger: German resentment, censorship,
poverty, illness and his Jewishness that was more than
just a religion.

What he has to say about communism is pro-
phetic, he saw it solely as an instrument of negation—
just as the inquisitor says to the delinquent, 'Show
him the instruments.' But he also saw what the party
of that name would do with them. No one listened
to him, of course.

Taking aim. Everyone who can handle a rowing boat, everyone who's shot a gun just once, every primary-school pupil who's been plagued with the parallelo-gram of forces knows how tricky it is to deal with more than one variable. The rower has to balance out the wind against the current, the marksman has to aim, taking the weight of the projectile and the move-ments of the target into account. If he shoots at the target, he'll miss it and hit something he wasn't aiming at.

In all social circumstances the number of vari-ables is much greater. That means the calculations facing every town councillor, every CEO, every shady lawyer demand a sure eye, practice and the ability to assess a situation. The difficulty increases the stronger the counterforces are compared to those at his disposal.

The movements in capitalist countries which are aiming to bring about revolutionary change, however, are unaware of that. In all innocence they identify their goal and head straight towards it. But as a rule their opponents don't stay where they've seen them. That is why political campaigns seldom achieve what they intend to, quite often the opposite. Ideology is the last thing to protect them against that.

In Germany the extra-parliamentary opposition and associated movements helped social democracy, they intended to combat, to come out on top. With

their agitation the Marxist–Leninists drew the attention of the unions to their most dangerous mistake
in the production process. The Red cells set the long
overdue structural reform of the universities in
motion. The left-wing playgroups tried out new ways
that educationalists didn't want to know about. Thus
the fundamental opposition to the whole system
merely helped to bring about its modernization. It did
more to give impetus to the learning process of capitalist society than the capitalists themselves.

The left-wing militants reacted to this by turning
even more radical. In the longer term, that helped
the regime they thought they were combating to
adapt more and more efficiently to the conditions of
globalization.

This blindness to the most simple rules governing
the mechanics of politics indicates, as does the belief
in the miracle-working power of ideological doc-
trines, the quasi-religious character of a movement in
which many parallels to the early socialism of the
nineteenth century can be seen.

Plans and more plans. So back to my desk. I worked
unabashed—not, as previously, behind the back of the
'movement' but quite openly. I was gathering the
material for a biography of Buenaventura Durruti. I
looked for traces of him in Spain, France, Holland and
filmed interviews with friendly old men who talked

about oppression, about armed resistance and about their defeats. I had to work out a separate structure for each version of the material (film, radio, book).

Then *Biography of a Runaway Slave* was on my desk, told by the slave himself and edited from recordings by Miguel Barnet. I even managed to meet the *Cimarrón from Cuba*, who was a 106 at the time. He said things such as, 'Most important of all is to remain calm. Without that a person can't live, can't think . . . That's not sad, for it's the truth.' That should be put on the stage, I thought. How about making a kind of libretto? Perhaps it would inspire Henze to write some music?

Or should we should just go ahead and see if we can make an opera?

In Germany dozens of theatres continue to put on *Die Fledermaus*, *Frau Luna* or something else by Strauss, Offenbach or Lehár, evening after evening. Operetta is regarded as an anachronistic mass medium. Why not a piece about the story of a government bond? For example, one based on the autobiography of the German banker, Carl Fürstenberg? Time and place correspond precisely to the heyday of the operetta that recorded the looting raids of capital on the Balkans done up in in fancy dress. Or on Leopold II, the king of Belgium who tore the heart out of Africa and ate up the flesh of his Congo Free State? At the conference of 1884, Bismarck and the representatives of the great powers let him have that prize. We could have Leopold, accompanied by his mistress, sing a triumphal aria in the bath, while in the anteroom his black lackeys wait for their wages. Is that not a subject for an operetta? Why shouldn't it work?

OK then. Let's stick to our own period. A vaudeville about the Cuban Revolution. Miguel Barnet has provided a draft for that as well: *Rachel's Song* (1995). Perhaps Henze, who is a friend of Miguel and knows everything about Cuban music, feels like taking on the story?

You could make a radio play out of the deaf Beethoven's conversation books, or resurrect a dark police comedy from the nineteenth century. The author, Sukhovo-Kobylin, even more maliciously witty than Labiche, is forgotten today. And some of Nikolai Erdman's plays have disappeared without trace as well. Meyerhold staged his *The Mandate* in 1925. Under Stalin he spent 20 years in the gulag and today I read in the paper that he has just died in Moscow, aged 70. I could also imagine a double psychodrama, about two communes: one would be set among IBM executives who have been sent to a castle not far from Amsterdam for sensitivity training, the other in a group of Maoists who squabble about their doctrine and the empty fridge.

And so on. What comes to the surface here—and will probably have no chance in the media market—is the pent-up desire to return to the things I like doing best.

Ulterior motives. Even as a child I knew that something of the kind existed. Things you keep to yourself. Thoughts that are never expressed, that mustn't congeal into words. The real motivating force is what lies behind them. There's northing mysterious about that.

That isn't possible in philosophy. A theory has to express what it has in mind, while literature leaves many things open. Good writers knows more than they say. Every reader understands the book in their own way. That means misunderstanding cannot be avoided; on the contrary, it's very welcome.

What is a classic? A work that has a long life because it contains possibilities that the author may not even have been aware of. He never was, never can be sole master of his creation. He does have to have some ability and that means he must be up to it technically, but at the same time he must have a remnant of naivety that evades the clutches of theory. Rationality and uninhibitedness cannot actually be combined. But that is precisely what gives literature its degree of freedom.

No one can say what all the things are that it may, should or must do. There are authors who do not feel it is their duty to change the world. When they're asked about it, they retort, 'Do as you like, but leave me in peace.' And they're quite within their rights. A writer who makes rules for other writers is an idiot.

Last chapter of a Russian novel. On that June day in Cambridge it was as if Lewis Carroll and his Alice could have been watching us. We were in a punt on the idyllic Cam. In 1972, Maria Alexandrovna had been appointed to a fellowship at King's College. I did wonder how that had come about. A woman in that convent for men, and a foreign one at that! Who had pulled the strings, in Moscow or elsewhere? Isaiah Berlin could well have had a hand in it. Or was it Lydia Chukovskaya? I didn't know the secrets of what went on behind the scenes.

From Russia Masha had brought a suitcase full of rare material. For years she had collected leaflets, manifestos, periodicals, volumes of poetry that were impossible to find, yellowing brochures from the great days of the avant-garde between 1915 and 1930. She intended to write a substantial scholarly work on them, far away from the noise of the present day.

Behind the magnificent gothic architecture, Cambridge was dominated by the uses and abuses of monastic life. The unwritten rules weren't easy to comprehend. In the college the doors and stairs creaked, the rooms were sparsely furnished, but at the same time the dons still enjoyed some remnants of medieval luxury. When asked, no one there could tell me how much a stamp for a letter cost. They simply handed their mail over to the silver-haired porter at the gate, who franked it. And a fellow didn't have to bother about his washing either.

But the tacit expectations were high. Anyone who didn't meet them ran the risk of being discreetly ostracized. Not a word would be said, but the academic world shows no mercy to failures. Shortly after that last love tryst Masha admitted to me, in the flat I'd rented for her in Battersea, that she had done nothing about her dissertation apart from making a few disconnected notes. Perhaps the standards she set herself were so high she was bound to fail. However that might be, her nerves were in tatters. Her scholarship was to end in a few weeks time and it was clear that her chances of success in the academic world were very poor. The evening ended in tears.

After that she just about managed to struggle through with Russian lessons and translations, got a part-time job at a university in Sussex and wrote a few articles for a superior film periodical.

As well as that, despite her falling out with her mother she kept popping up in Moscow, bringing gifts from the inaccessible West and charming her friends with her cosmopolitan ways. But she could no longer settle down in such an environment. I heard that ultimately she held far-left views and was much taken with the Proletkult. One of the leading figures of that Russian writers' organization of the 1920s was the awful Fadeyev, Masha's biological father, whom she never met. In 1932 the Central Committee decided to dissolve the association, which called itself RAPP. Fadeyev couldn't wait to distance himself from his companions and expressed regret for his previous errors. Could it be that Masha had the idea of taking belated intellectual revenge on her father?

There was no danger in that, for there was no lack of friends in London who adopted a radical air and were far to the left of the Labour Party. Someone told me she was a brilliant hostess; the *New Left* held quite a few parties in her flat. I didn't find that difficult to believe. The English intellectuals I was acquainted with were highly intelligent, cosmopolitan people, journalists, professors, film-makers and translators. But I doubt whether they ever had to do with a woman like Masha. She probably inspired them with desire and fear in equal proportions. Perhaps they suspected that behind her fiery appearance there were things that they found unsettling: loneliness, unhappiness and failure. There was still something glimmering inside her, even if she didn't have much time left.

We only saw each other once more. I'm afraid that on both sides it had come to a kind of weary fatigue. But a Russian novel cannot end in dull silence.

A dramatic scene is essential, at night, if possible, or in the first light of dawn. A woman like Masha was not to be denied her final row. An *amour fou* is a battle in which there can be neither victor nor vanquished.

I last saw Maria Alexandrovna Enzensberger, née Makarova, in London in 1979. One year later we were divorced. I did manage to acquire a flat in Highgate for her but I never set foot in it. In the autumn of 1991, one day before the birthday of her mother, with whom she had been never reconciled, Masha took her own life. She wasn't the first; her elder sister Tanya had died a long time ago in a state of alcoholic delirium

Margarita Iosifovna Aliger, who was spared nothing in her life, wrote to me in the summer of 1971, after Masha and I had separated:

Thank you for your letter, for its sad clarity. God, how sad it is. The poor girl, the stupid girl, the little girl. And it's no one's fault, no one can do anything about it. But you're quite right, it is quite clear that there's no point in brooding over it. I very much regret that we didn't see each other often enough and talked so little. I was convinced we still had our whole lives in front of us. Pity that wasn't the case. I sometimes feel that in comparison with my daughters, I am a very simple, very ordinary person, even very primitive. For that reason there are unfortunately many things I can't understand. Be happy. Don't forget me. I will always be glad to welcome you in my house.

I was fortunate enough to see her again, in the summer of 1976. Her eyesight was going. The doctors were talking of incurable macular degeneration. She could only read with the help of a cumbersome pair of glasses with yellow lenses. I managed to persuade her to come to Munich, where there's a good eye clinic and special glasses for such cases. Margarita died in August 1992, one year after her daughter Masha, in Mitschurinets near Peredelkino.

Poor Heberto Padilla finally managed, with the help of Edward Kennedy, to leave Cuba in 1980. His life in the USA was unhappy. He did produce a novel and poems, but he never recovered from the public humiliation. His wife, Belkis, left him, he drank too much and had a heart attack from which he died in September 2000, in Auburn, a small town in the east of Alabama.

There is a detailed documentation of the 'Padilla Affair' in *Libre, Volume 1* (1971), pp. 93–145.

Herbert Marcuse died in 1979, in Starnberg, where he was visiting Jürgen Habermas.

A more extensive account of Baader, Meinhof & Co. can be found in a conversation with Jan Philipp Reemtsma and Wolfgang Kraushaar (ed.), *Die RAF und der linke Terrorismus*, Volume 2 (2006), pp. 1392–1411.

Reinhard Lettau died, after a long illness, in 1996 in Karlsruhe. His grave is next to that of E. T. A. Hoffmann in Berlin.

REMEMBRANCE

(1978)

So as far as the sixties are concerned,
I can be brief.
Enquiries was always engaged.
The miracle of the loaves and fishes
was restricted to Düsseldorf and its environs.
The terrible news came over the telex,
was noted and archived.
The seventies
swallowed themselves up,
unresisting by and large,
with no guarantee for later generations,
Turks and the unemployed.
That anyone should think of them with consideration
would be asking too much.